TO YOUR ETERNITY

YOSHITOKI OIMA

9

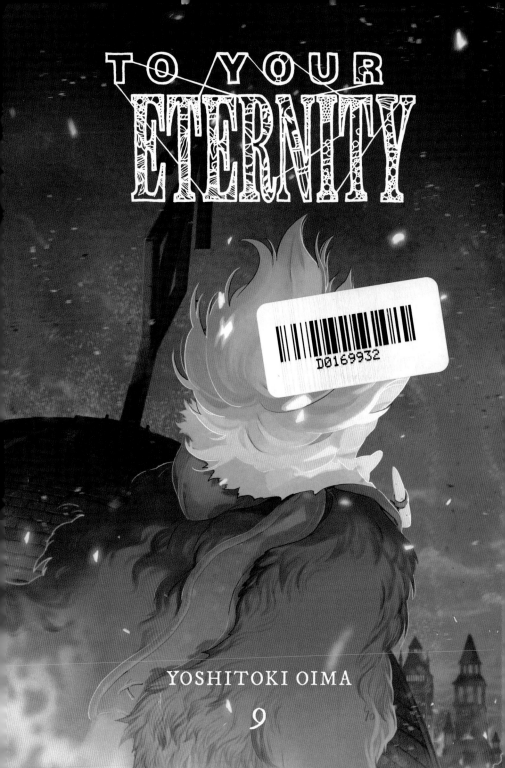

CONTENTS

#75 Punishment and Pardon 3
#76 Beyond the Dream 23
#77 Fantasy and Reality 43
#78 The Curtain Pulled Back 61
#79 The Black Flames of War 81
#80 A Tireless Enemy 99
#81 Spreading Consciousness 117
#82 Bet on the Future 135
#83 Control 153
#84 Resonance 171

SKREEEEEK
#75 Punishment and Pardon
FUSHI!!

ZWISH!!

WHOA!!

CRUNCH

WHUMP

DID YOU COME TO SAVE US, FUSHI?!

GRAH!

LET'S RUN, BON.

T-TAKE THIS BOY FIRST.

KREEEK
COME ON, BON. YOU, TOO.

W-WAIT A SECOND. EVEN IF WE RUN AWAY, THE CHURCH OF BENNETT WON'T GIVE UP.
NOT A PROBLEM.
THEY HAVEN'T NOTICED ANYTHING.
THEY THINK I'VE BEEN PERMANENTLY SEALED IN METAL.
SHWIP

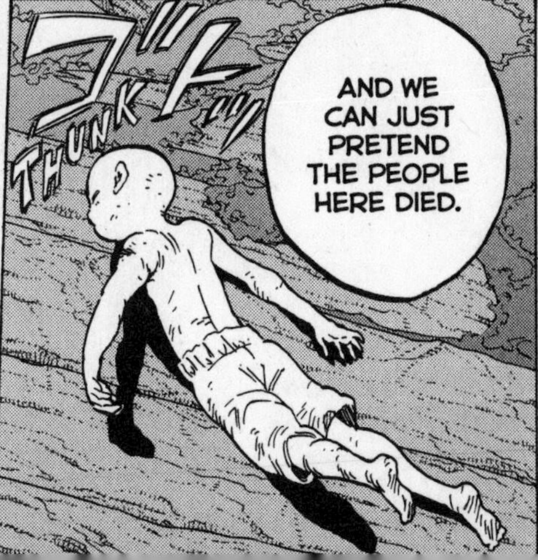
THUNK
AND WE CAN JUST PRETEND THE PEOPLE HERE DIED.

NOW, GET IN, BON.

WH-
WHY?

I'LL STAY HERE.

CYLIRA AND THE OTHERS' OBJECTIVE IS TO SHOW THE CITIZENS THAT FUSHI IS A SERVANT OF THE DEVIL.
I KNOW THAT'S WHY I WAS CAPTURED.
NOT TO PUNISH A SINNER, BUT TO MAKE HIM ADMIT HIS SIN.
IF I DIE HERE, THEY WON'T GET THE ENDING THEY WANT.
SPLASH
SPLASH

AND THEY'LL KEEP UP THEIR SILLY HERETIC HUNT UNTIL THEY'RE FINALLY SATISFIED.
THEY'LL GO AFTER MY FAMILY, MY SERVANTS, TODO, THE GUARDIANS... EVERYONE WHO LOVES YOU...
I ALONE *MUST* STAY HERE AND ACCOMPLISH THEIR TRIAL. ONLY THEN CAN I LEAVE.

B...
BUT CAN YOU BE SAVED THAT WAY?

YES.
AS LONG AS I GET THEIR PARDON.
PARDON?

BY ACKNOWL-EDGING THAT YOU...
...ARE A SERVANT OF THE DEVIL.

THEY CAN ACCEPT THE EXISTENCE OF THE DEVIL. WHAT THEY CAN'T ACCEPT IS SOMEONE WHO CAN BE REVERED AS A NEW GOD.

C-CYLIRA SAID THEY'LL RELEASE ME IF I ADMIT MY SIN.

SORRY, FUSHI...

WHAT-
EVER KEEPS
YOU ALIVE.
THAT'S WHAT
I'M IN FAVOR
OF.

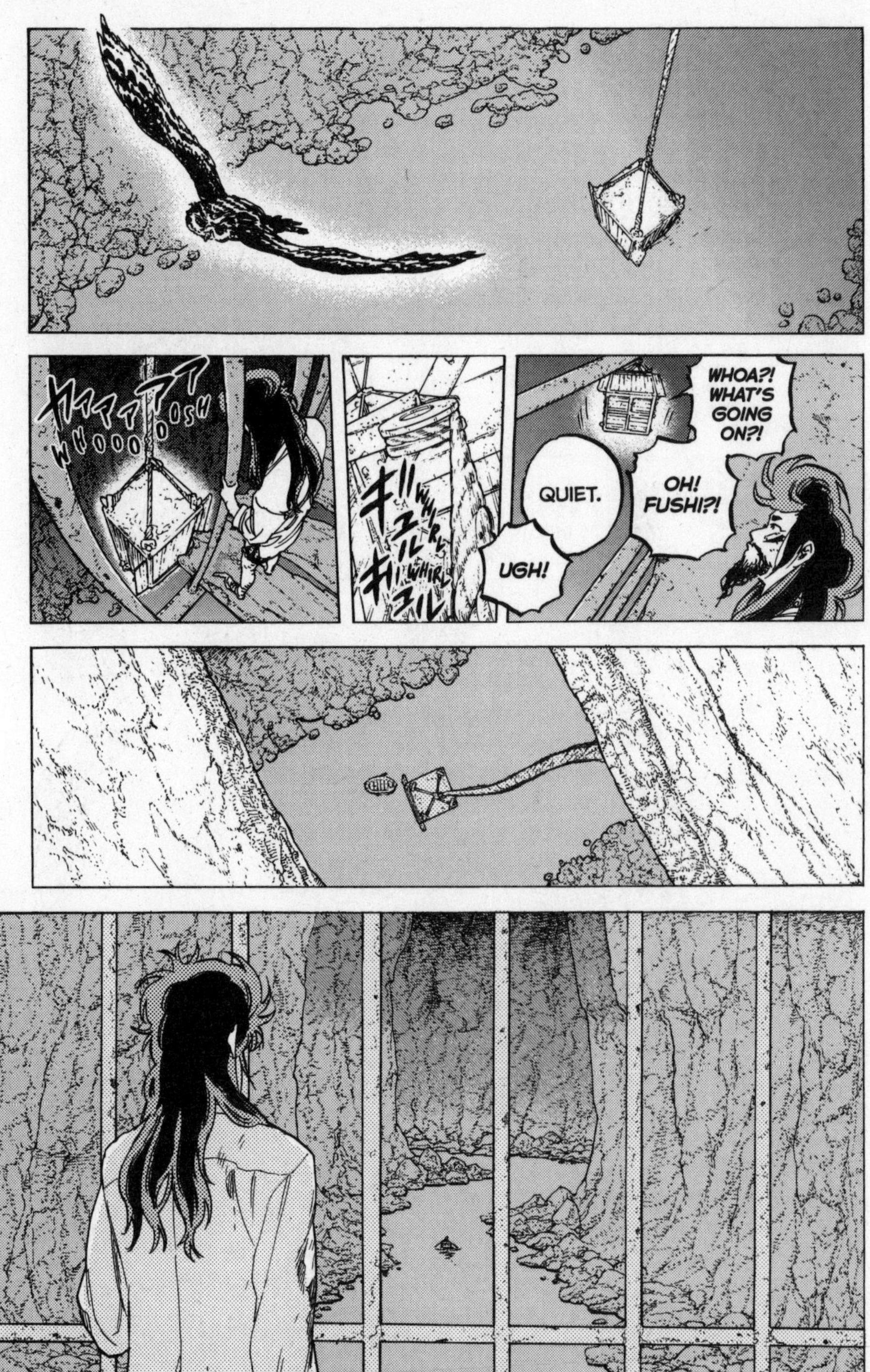
WHOA?! WHAT'S GOING ON?!
OH! FUSHI?!
QUIET.
UGH!
キュルキュル
WHIRL WHIRL
カァァァァ
WHOOOOOOSH

THAT WAS VERY NOBLE OF YOU, PRINCE.

YES, TRULY.

TWO DEAD IN ONE NIGHT...

THE BARS WERE DESTROYED ...

WH-WHAT IN THE WORLD...

...HAPPENED HERE?

OH.

A DEVIL CAME AND TOOK THEIR LIVES.

IT MUST NOT'VE BEEN ABLE TO TAKE MINE BECAUSE GOD WAS WITH ME.

HERE'S THE TRUTH...

THAT DEVIL KNEW I COULD SEE IT, SO IT GAVE ME A MESSAGE.

THAT'S WHEN I SAID, "WHO'D DO A FAVOR FOR THE DEVIL?"

THE DEVIL SAID, "IF YOU DON'T, THEN THIS IS WHAT WILL HAPPEN TO YOU." THEN IT TOOK THEIR SOULS AND FLEW AWAY.

"HOW DARE YOU SEAL MY COMRADE IN METAL?!"

"BUT THIS IS THE LAST TIME."

"IN THE FUTURE, IF YOU TAKE INTEREST IN US AGAIN, WE WILL KILL YOU."

SO, IN SHORT, BONCHIEN...

YOU WITNESSED PROOF THAT FUSHI IS A DEVIL.

...

YEAH.

DO YOU ADMIT THAT FUSHI CONSORTS WITH DEVILS?

...

YEAH.

NO.

I LOVE FUSHI!

THERE... EVERYTHING IS GOING WELL.

I WAS THE HAPPIEST MAN IN THE KINGDOM...
BECAUSE I THOUGHT EVERYTHING I SAW WOULD BE MINE.

THE THRONE...
FUSHI...

AND, IN ORDER TO GET THEM, I THREW QUITE A TANTRUM.

DESPITE MY POWERS, I COULD NOT FACE THE TRUTH SO EVIDENT BEFORE ME. I WAS A COWARD.

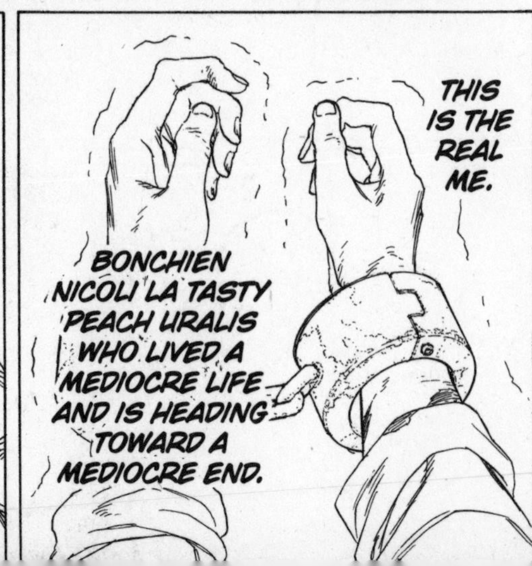
THIS IS THE REAL ME.
BONCHIEN NICOLI LA TASTY PEACH URALIS WHO LIVED A MEDIOCRE LIFE AND IS HEADING TOWARD A MEDIOCRE END.

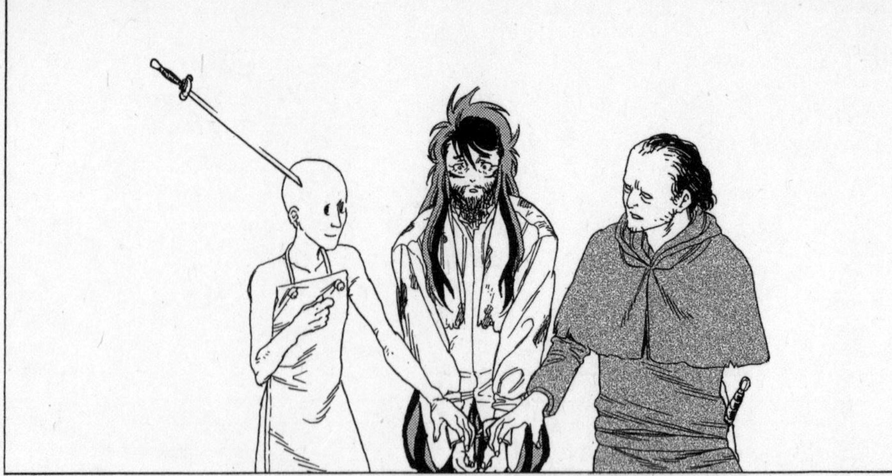

IN LIFE, I WAS A MERE BEGGAR THAT LIVED ABOVE THE CEILING OF THE CASTLE AND WOULD SNEAK INTO THE KITCHEN TO FILL MY BELLY.
THAT DAY, I DIDN'T EVEN NOTICE THE CASTLE WAS UNDER ATTACK. WHILE I WAS STUFFING MY FACE, SOMEONE STABBED ME IN THE HEAD...

AS FOR ME, I GOT MY LEFT ARM CUT OFF BEFORE I COULD PROTECT EVEN A SINGLE SOUL.
NO ONE STOPPED TO MEND MY WOUND, AND I DIED.

THOSE ARE MEDIOCRE ENDS.
WHAT...?
YES.
I DON'T KNOW OF ANY-ONE WHO MADE A CHOICE AS NOBLE AS YOURS, PRINCE...

YOU LIED TO FUSHI, DIDN'T YOU?
YOU HAD NO INTENTION OF TRYING TO SAVE YOURSELF.
YOU PROTECTED FUSHI AND THE CITIZENS BY PLAYING THE VILLAIN AND LETTING THE CHURCH BE THE HERO.

WE WILL NOW COMMENCE THE EXECUTION OF BONCHIEN NICOLI LA TASTY PEACH URALIS.

TO YOUR
ETERNITY

TO YOUR
ETERNITY

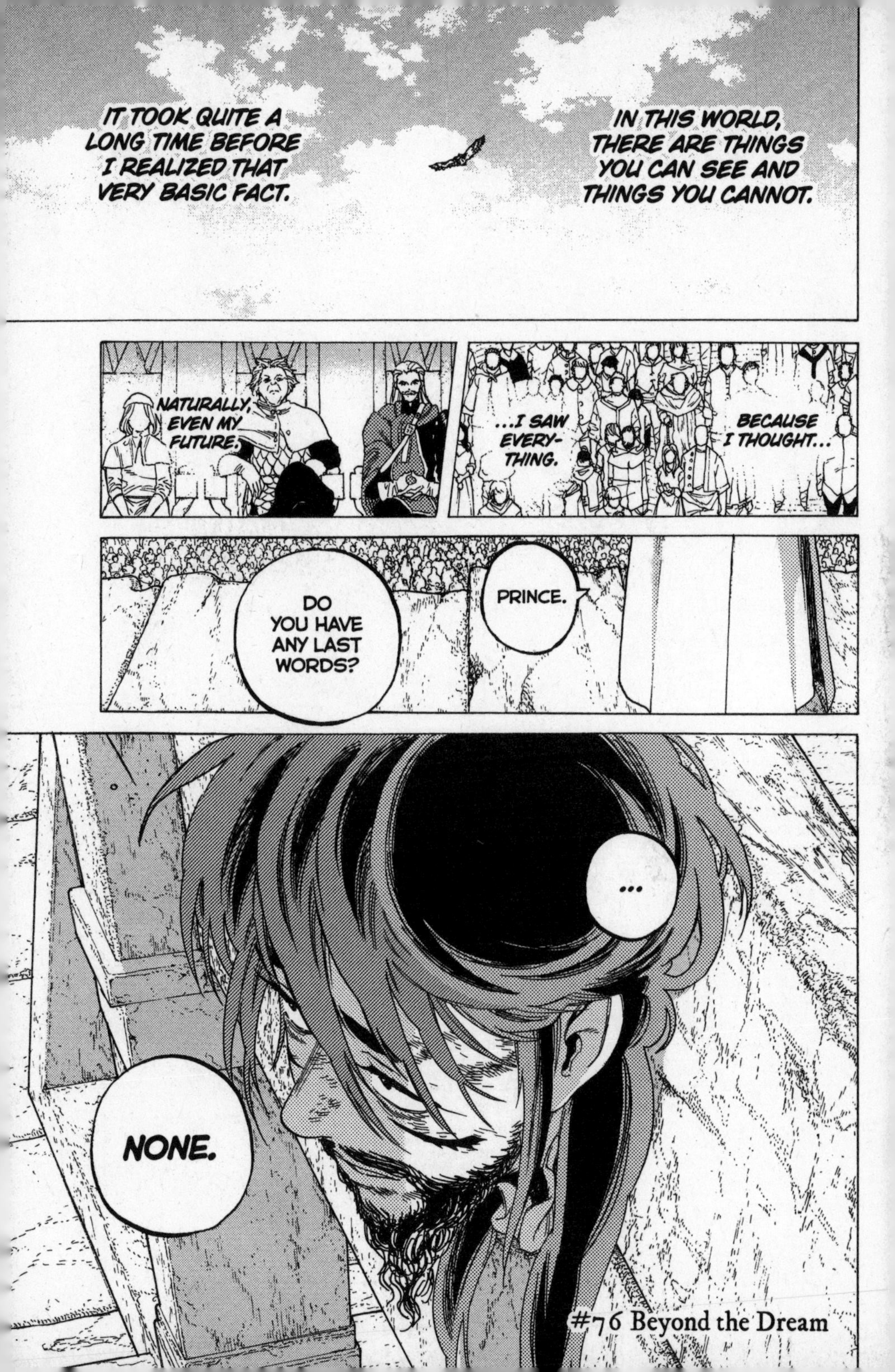

IN THIS WORLD, THERE ARE THINGS YOU CAN SEE AND THINGS YOU CANNOT.

IT TOOK QUITE A LONG TIME BEFORE I REALIZED THAT VERY BASIC FACT.

BECAUSE I THOUGHT...
...I SAW EVERY-THING.
NATURALLY, EVEN MY FUTURE.
PRINCE.
DO YOU HAVE ANY LAST WORDS?

...

NONE.

#76 Beyond the Dream

I AM BONCHIEN NICOLI LA TASTY PEACH URALIS.

IT'S BEGINNING TO RAIN.

I AM ABOUT TO DIE.

LET'S BEGIN.

PAPA...
I'M SORRY I DISAPPOINTED YOU.

MAMA...
YOU WON'T HAVE TO WORRY ABOUT ME ANYMORE.

POCOA...
TRY TO BRIGHTEN UP THE CASTLE AFTER I'M GONE.

TORTA...
THE KINGDOM OF URALIS IS IN YOUR HANDS. I'M SURE YOU CAN HANDLE IT.

FUSHI... IT WAS AN HONOR MEETING YOU.

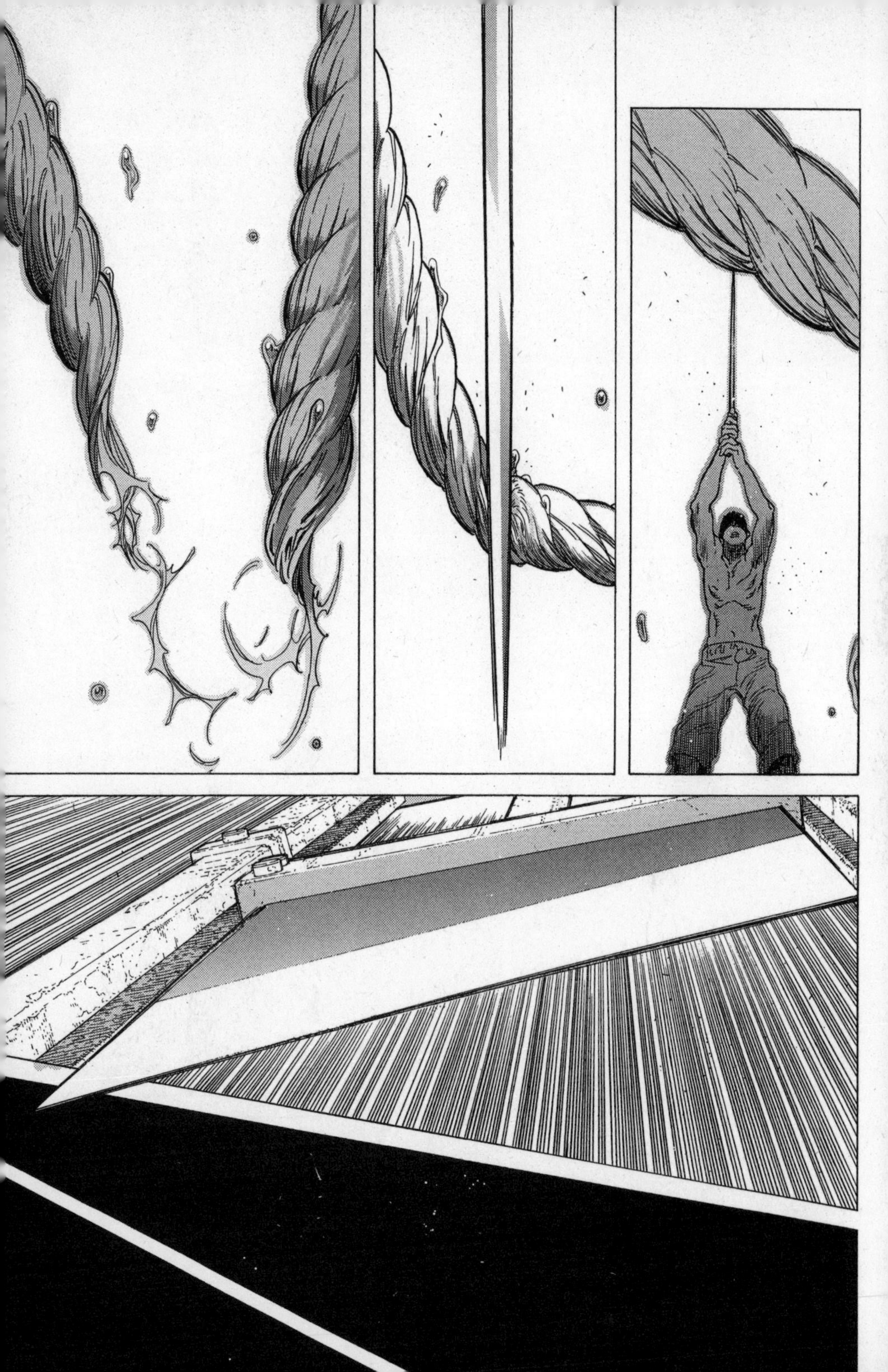

ELDER CYLIRA!
ELDER CYLIRA!
PLEASE WAKE UP!
UGH...

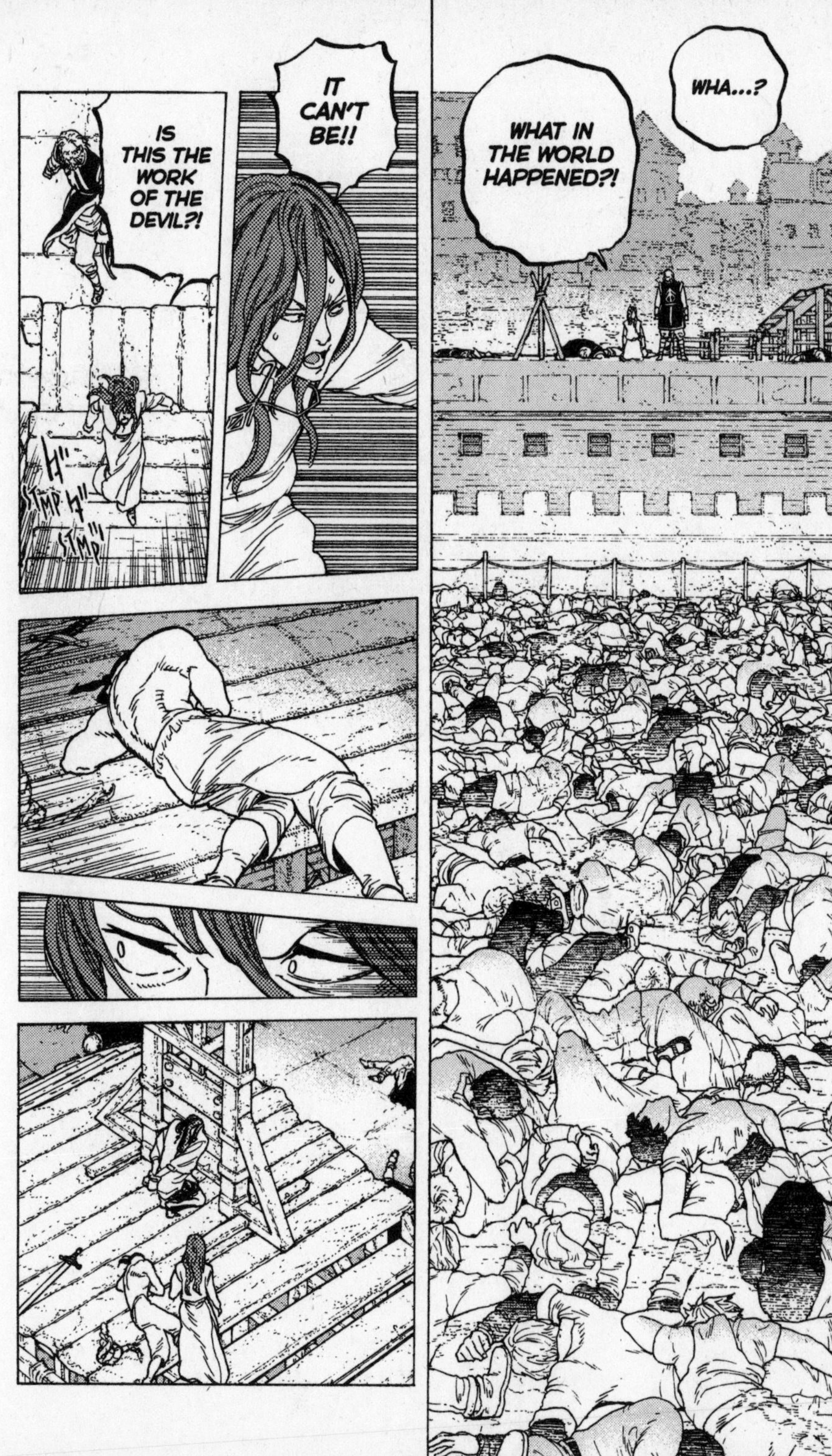
WHA...?
WHAT IN THE WORLD HAPPENED?!
IT CAN'T BE!!
IS THIS THE WORK OF THE DEVIL?!
STMP STMP

THE EXECUTION WAS A SUCCESS, ELDER CYLIRA!
THE DEVIL WAS TOO LATE!!
WE WON!

WHAT?!

BON IS
DEAD?!

PRINCE.

PRINCE BON.

YOU TWO...
AM I...
...DEAD?
THE PRINCE NAMED BON IS DEAD.
YES.
OH...
THEN WHERE AM I?
OH!
I'M GLAD YOU'RE AWAKE, BON!
THIS IS URALIS.
TODO AND THE BOY ARE ALL RIGHT, TOO.
THEY'RE IN A PLACE WHERE NO ONE WILL FIND THEM.
F-FUSHI?!
WAIT HERE! I'LL GET YOU SOME NEW CLOTHES.

WAIT, FUSHI! YOU CAN SEE ME?
BUT I'M DEAD!!
WHAT ARE YOU TALKING ABOUT, BON?
THE OLD YOU DIED, BUT YOU'RE STILL ALIVE.
HUH?!

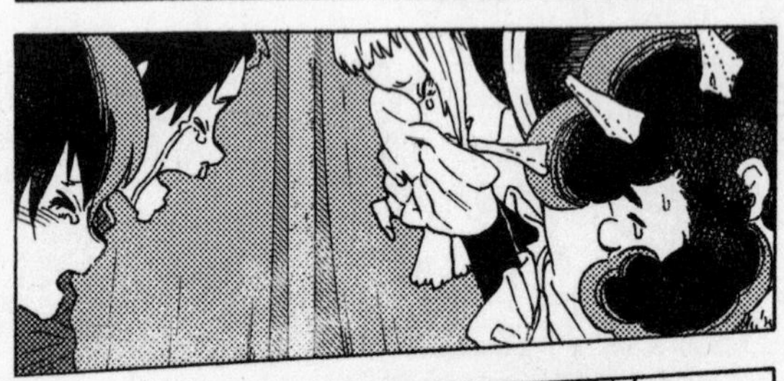

OH! I GET IT!!
DIDN'T THE YANOME SAY... THE DEAD CAN HAVE THEIR WISHES COME TRUE?!
SO THIS WORLD WAS INFLUENCED BY MY WISHES!
OH YEAH. I'VE HEARD THAT STORY A FEW TIMES.
BUT IF THAT WERE TRUE, WOULDN'T YOU BE KING?

BROTHER?!

BON!!

BIG BROTHER!!

EVERY-ONE!!

WHUMP

FUSHI, WHAT THE DEVIL DID YOU DO?

I BELIEVED IN YOU WHEN YOU SAID YOU'D STAY BEHIND.
BUT THAT WASN'T REASON ENOUGH FOR ME TO DESERT YOU.
I STARTED WORKING ON A PLAN AS SOON AS I GOT BACK TO THE BASE, BUT I COULDN'T COME UP WITH A GOOD ONE ON MY OWN.
THEN, SOMEONE GAVE ME A HINT.
TONARI'S ORIGINAL DIARY CONTAINS DETAILS NOT INCLUDED IN THE PUBLISHED VERSION.
WHEN I LOOKED, THERE WAS INFORMATION ABOUT ALL SORTS OF POISONS AND MEDICINES SLIPPED INTO THE MAIN TEXT.

IT IS FINISHED.
THIS IS THE ULTIMATE SLEEPING POTION.
GLUG GLUG GLUG
URP!
GULP
HUFF
PUFF
IT TASTED HORRIBLE.
BLUB
BLUB
SO I WAS ABLE TO RE-CREATE IT RIGHT AWAY.

THEN I TURNED INTO LIGARD AND SPREAD IT FROM ABOVE.
I JUST BARELY MADE IT IN TIME.

ALL I HAD TO DO THEN WAS CREATE A COPY OF YOUR BODY AND MAKE IT LOOK LIKE YOU DIED.

THAT WAS THE ONLY WAY I COULD TAKE YOU AWAY... WILL YOU FORGIVE ME, BON?

FORGIVE YOU? FOR WHAT?
THERE MIGHT'VE BEEN A BETTER WAY.
NOW, EVERYONE THINKS YOU'RE DEAD.
AND A BUNCH OF PEOPLE WERE SADDENED BY THAT.

WHAT ARE YOU SAYING, FUSHI? THIS WAS THE BEST POSSIBLE OUTCOME FOR ME!
EVEN BETTER THAN BECOMING KING!

BETTER THAN BEING KING?
YES. I'M NOT DREAMING, AM I, FUSHI?

I'VE NEVER BEEN HAPPIER TO NOT BE KING IN MY LIFE!

THANK YOU FOR SAVING ME, FUSHI.

...

...I...

...SAVED YOU?

TO YOUR
ETERNITY

In the city of Entas, our great sage Cylira finally captured the devil Fushi, who falsely claimed to be a servant of god in order to lead the people astray.

Following the laws of Bennett, the devil Fushi was locked in a metal prison, which was then filled with molten iron.

A few weeks later, the devil Fushi used his wicked powers to destroy this prison and attempted to show himself before us, but the sage Cylira's resourcefulness and the holy water of Bennett allowed us to successfully seal him again.

Since that day, not a single soul has seen Fushi.

WORKS OF THE SAINTS THE BOOK OF ST. CYLIRA

THE SEALING OF THE DEVIL FUSHI

#77 Fantasy and Reality

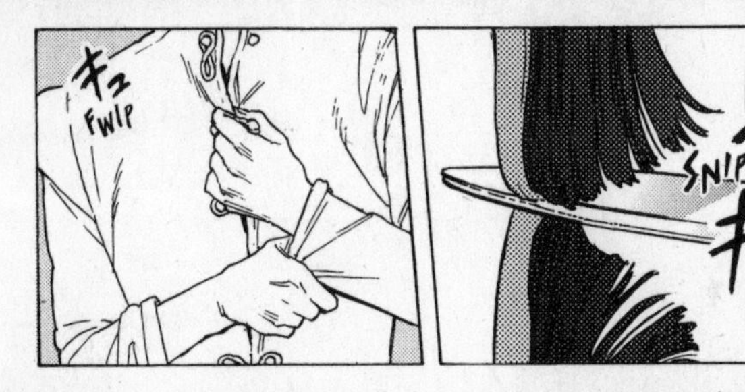

YOU CERTAINLY CLEANED UP NICE.

YOU HAVEN'T SEEN TODO AND THE OTHERS YET, HAVE YOU?

THEY ARE HAVING TEA BELOW.

THEY ARE IN THE GARDEN BELOW THERE.

BUT THEY ARE ATTRACTING A LOT OF ATTENTION, SO PLEASE BE CAREFUL.

FOR ME, IT'S THE GIRL ON THE LEFT! NO QUESTION!

THEN THE ONE IN THE MIDDLE'S MINE!!

I'VE GOTTA GO WITH LADY POCOA~

WHAT ARE YOU FELLOWS DOING?

LADY POCOA'S FRIENDS ARE VISITING!!

WHICH ONE'S YOUR TYPE?

THE SHECRET TO DIETING IS DEFINITELY NOT EATING!!

YES, EXACTLY.

I COULD NEVER DO ANYTHING SO HARD.

BY THE WAY, DID YOU DECIDE ON A NAME FOR YOUR HORSEY?
HUH? HORSE?
A GUY LIKE ME— I MEAN... UM, YOU WOULD ALLOW ME TO CHOOSE?
OF COURSHE! WE GAVE IT TO YOU, SO IT'S YOURSH NOW!
WHOA!
I'M AFRAID THIS AREA'S OFF-LIMITS WITHOUT PERMISSION.
HMM?!
WHAT WOULD BE A GOOD NAME?
WHY NOT THE NAME OF SOME-THING YOU LIKE?
LIKE THE NAME OF A FOOD?
BISCUIT!!
HOW ABOUT PEACH TEA?
LIL LEMON CAKE!
I WANT A COOLER NAME.
WAIT A MINUTE...
I'VE SEEN YOUR FACE BEFORE...
HUH? YOU THINK SO?

AH!
BIG BROTHER!
HUH?
SOME-THING ABOUT YOU SMELLS...
YOU'RE IMAGINING THINGS.
...'S!
...FRIEND...
DO YOU KNOW THIS MAN, LADY POCOA?
YES... HE WAS A FRIEND OF MY BROTHER'SH...
SPRING ROLL!
BARON SPRING-ROLL!
HAHA, IS THAT SO? I KNEW HE SMELLED AWFULLY HIGH-CLASS.
IT'S THE GUY WE JUST SAW.
WHO IS HE?
APPARENTLY, HE WAS ONE OF MASTER BON'S FRIENDS.

LET ME INTRODUCE YOU! GIRLS, THISH IS BARON SPRINGROLL!

GASP! は,

NICE TO MEET YOU...
SHE TOOK IT! SPRING ROLL WAS MY IDEA!

AND THESE LADIES ARE IRIS AND JOAAN.

OH! CHABO... THAT BOY LEFT TO EXPLORE THE KITCHEN...
WHY DON'T YOU GO SEE HIM...?

...
ALL RIGHT.

WHY DON'T YOU SHOW ME...IT?
YOU KNOW, THE THING YOU WERE MAKING WITH THREAD?
HMM?
HUH?
OH!
WHAT-EVER DO YOU MEAN?
OH.
ISN'T HE TALKING ABOUT THAT HANDKER-CHIEF?
YOU BOUGHT THAT THREAD BEFORE. OH! DID YOU WANT ME TO KEEP QUIET ABOUT THAT?
UGH...
...

HERE...
FOR YOU...

WOW! YOU'RE GOOD!
H-HOW DID YOU MAKE THIS? SHOW ME SOMETIME!

YES... IT'S WELL-MADE.

HEHEH...
AHAHA!

OH, YES.
DON'T YOU HAVE ANOTHER? THE ONE I CARRIED BEFORE.

OH, THAT ONE? YES, I STILL HAVE IT.
RUSTLE RUSTLE

...
YES, YOU REALLY *ARE* GOOD...

TH-THANK YOU.

HAHA!
ガタッ
THUNK

HAHA!
HA! HA! HA! HA!
WHERE'RE YOU GOING?
SIGH, I'M GOING TO REST FOR A BIT.

HA! HA!
HA! HA!
WANT SOME MORE, KIDDO?
YEAH.

MISTER?
CREAK

EAT THIS.
CHABBY...
IT'LL MAKE YOU FEEL BETTER.
YOU'RE SO KIND.

I'LL EAT IT WHEN I FEEL BETTER...
HOW WEIRD...
BARON SPRING-ROLL.
THIS IS PRINCE BON'S ROOM, SO YOU SHOULDN'T USE IT.

IF I WERE PRINCE BON, I'D ALLOW IT!! SO IT'S FINE!!
WHAT THE DEVIL IS ALL THIS, FUSHI? ...I MEAN, JOAAN.

U-UM, H-HAVE I DONE SOMETHING RUDE...?

CAN I ASK YOU SOME- THING?

Y-YES.

WE MET WHEN WE WERE YOUNGER, DIDN'T WE?

...
YES.

WHAT WERE YOU HERE FOR THEN?
...HELP- ING MY FATHER.
HE'S A TAILOR...
ALTHOUGH HE GOT FIRED SHORTLY THERE- AFTER...

FIRED?
YES... THERE WAS A RULE IN THE CASTLE THAT GIRLS FROM THE OUTSIDE LIKE ME WEREN'T ALLOWED TO SPEAK TO THE PRINCE.
IT WAS APPARENTLY REPORTED TO THE QUEEN THAT I TRIED TO SEDUCE YOU...

AND THEN...
...YOU GAVE ME THIS?
HOW DID YOU SNEAK IN?

I LOOKED UP ROUTES THE GUARDS WOULDN'T SEE...
...AND SCALED THE WALL.

...AND YOU PUT ON ALL THAT WEIGHT AFTER-WARDS?
YES! A DELICIOUS SWEET SHOP OPENED ON OUR STREET!

CHOMP
CHOMP

WHY DID YOU RETURN TO THE CASTLE?

I...
I WAS JUST SO HAPPY...
...THAT YOU FOUND ME ALL THOSE YEARS AGO...
...SO SINCE THEN I'VE...

SHE WAS NEAT, AND GRACEFUL, LOVELY!!
STOP MAKING THINGS UP!!
SH-SH-SHE WOULD NEVER SCALE A WALL, OR GET AS FAT AS A PIG, OR ACT AS A HUMAN CHAIR, OR DIVE INTO A FILTHY PILE OF DUNG!!
SLAM!!
IRIS?!
WHAT JUST HAP-PENED?
THAT WAS JUST AS BAD AS PRINCE BON'S SELF-ISHNESS.
WAIT!

HEY, WHADDA YOU THINK YOU'RE DOING, IRIS?!
I!
JUST DECIDED TO TURN BACK INTO A MAN!!
CHOMP
CHOMP
BUT YOU JUST LOSHT ALL THAT WEIGHT!! HAVE YOU LOSHT YOUR MIND ?!
APPARENTLY, *THAT MAN* GETS IN A SOUR MOOD WHEN I'M THIN!
STOP THAT!!
DON'T FORGET.
THE BRAVE WARRIOR TODO IS DEAD.
"A GALLANT MAN WHO FOUGHT TO DEFEND THE PRINCE'S LIFE."

IF THE PRINCE WERE STILL ALIVE, I'M SURE HE WOULD SAY...

THANK YOU FOR SAVING ME.

BA'BANG

BANG

IRIS?!
F-FATHER?!

I'M SO GLAD YOU'RE ALL RIGHT!!
WHEN I HEARD YOU HAD DIED, I...!!
I'M SORRY I WORRIED YOU!!
DID YOU CALL HIM?
YES.

ARE YOU GOING TO...GO HOME?

WHAT DO YOU THINK, IRIS?
WILL THEY LET YOU SERVE HERE IN THE CASTLE AS YOU HAVE IN THE PAST?
OR DO YOU WANT TO RETURN WITH ME TO THE CITY?

HUH...?

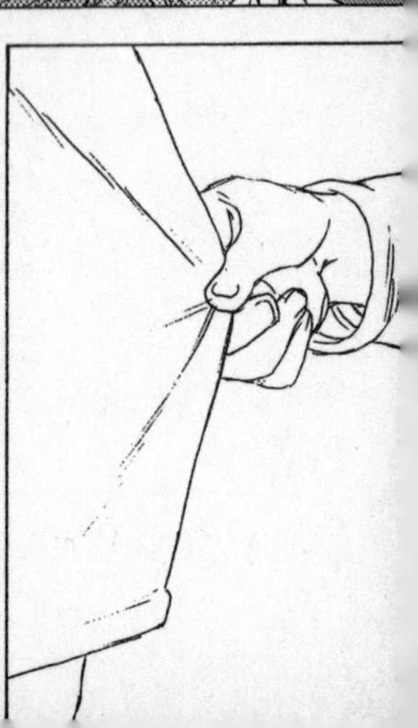

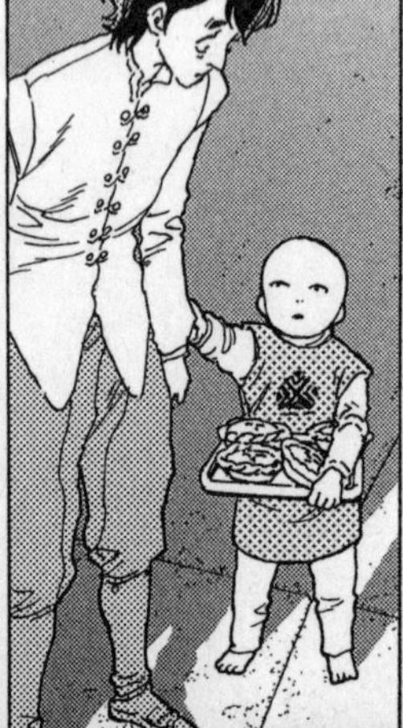

HEY.
I'M NOT GONNA END UP ALONE, AM I?

OF COURSE NOT, CHABBY!
WE'LL LOOK AFTER YOU!

THAT MAKES US SOUND KINDA LIKE A FAMILY...

F-FAMILY?! DON'T BE SILLY!
I-I MEAN! HE HATES ME!

TH-THAT ISN'T TRUE! THAT'S NOT WHAT I MEANT!
THEN WHAT DID YOU MEAN?!

THE REAL YOU WAS SIMPLY SO DIFFERENT FROM WHAT I'D IMAGINED... THAT MY WORD CHOICE...
WHAT DOES THAT MATTER TO YOU?!
C-CAN'T YOU TELL?
NO, I CAN'T TELL!
OH, THEN NEVER MIND.

WHAT DO YOU MEAN "NEVER MIND" ?!
CHOMP
OKAY, FINE. I'LL TELL YOU.

I'M SORRY I SAID THOSE MEAN THINGS.

I WANT YOU TO STAY HERE IN THE CASTLE FOREVER.

OKAY!

THE DEATH OF THE PRINCE OF URALIS.

AND THE IMMORTAL WHO BECAME A LEGEND.

#78 The Curtain Pulled Back

I, THE MORE SUBDUED OF US, LEARNED MUCH FROM MY BROTHER.
HE LOVED HAPPY, BEAUTIFUL THINGS AND SHOWED US THE TRUE MEANING OF JUSTICE...

MASTER BON!!
THANK YOU!

YES, I KNOW WHAT YOU MEAN.
SO DO I.

WHAT DO YOU THINK?

...YES.
...YES.

YOU THINK SO?
YES, I THINK YOU'RE RIGHT.

I'M READY.
WHO WERE YOU TALKING TO?

HMM?
NO, IT'S JUST MY USUAL MALADY.

WELL, EVERY-ONE...
THANK YOU FOR ALL YOU'VE DONE FOR ME.

YEAH.
PLEASE COME BACK SOMEDAY.

EVEN WITH FUSHI AND BON GONE, I PLAN TO KEEP PROTECTING THE PEOPLE FROM NOKKERS.
DO YOU FEEL THE SAME WAY?
OF COURSE.

I THINK BON SAID SOMETHING ABOUT REWARDING YOU.
I REMEM-BER.
YOU ENRICHED HIS HEART.
I DID?
I WANT TO REWARD YOU IN HIS STEAD, BUT I'D ALSO LIKE TO BE CAREFUL.

SO LET ME ASK... *IF THE FRIENDS YOU MET ALONG THE WAY...*
...WERE IMMORTAL, WOULD YOU BE HAPPY?

WELL-

OW!
WHAT'S THE MATTER?!

SOME-ONE'S PAIN...
I FELT IT FROM OVER THERE...

WAIT, WHERE'S KAHAKU ...?

I HAVEN'T SEEN HIM SINCE THIS MORNING...

KAHAKU?
CREEAK

FUSHI WAS DECLARED A DEVIL... AND IT WAS MY FAULT THAT EVERYTHING WENT AWRY...

AND WHAT'S MORE, THE WOMAN I LOVED HATES ME, SO I WILL NOT BE ABLE TO HAVE CHILDREN, AND THE GUARDIANS ARE DONE FOR...

"DON'T KILL ME."

SKRITCH...
"FUSHI SAID TO LEARN TO TALK..."
"...AND WHILE I CANNOT SPEAK YET..."

ARE YOU SCREWING WITH US?
ABSO-LUTELY NOT!

SKRITCH
CRUNCH CRUNCH

"...I LEARNED AS BEST AS I COULD."

HUH.
YOU'RE PRETTY CUTE, EH?

IF YOU DON'T WANNA DIE, THEN ANSWER ME.
WHAT ARE YOUR—THE NOKKERS—GOALS?

"TO SAVE EVERYONE."

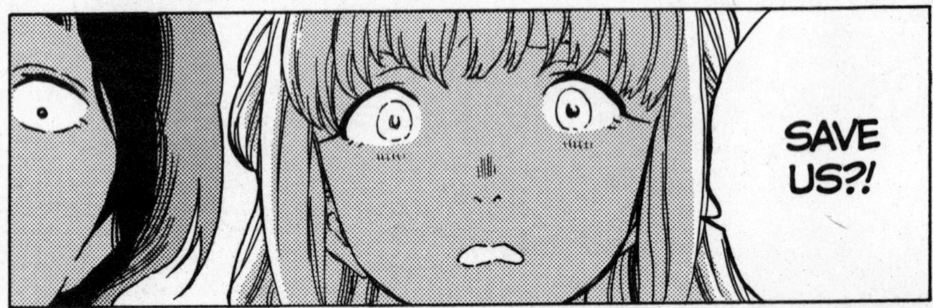

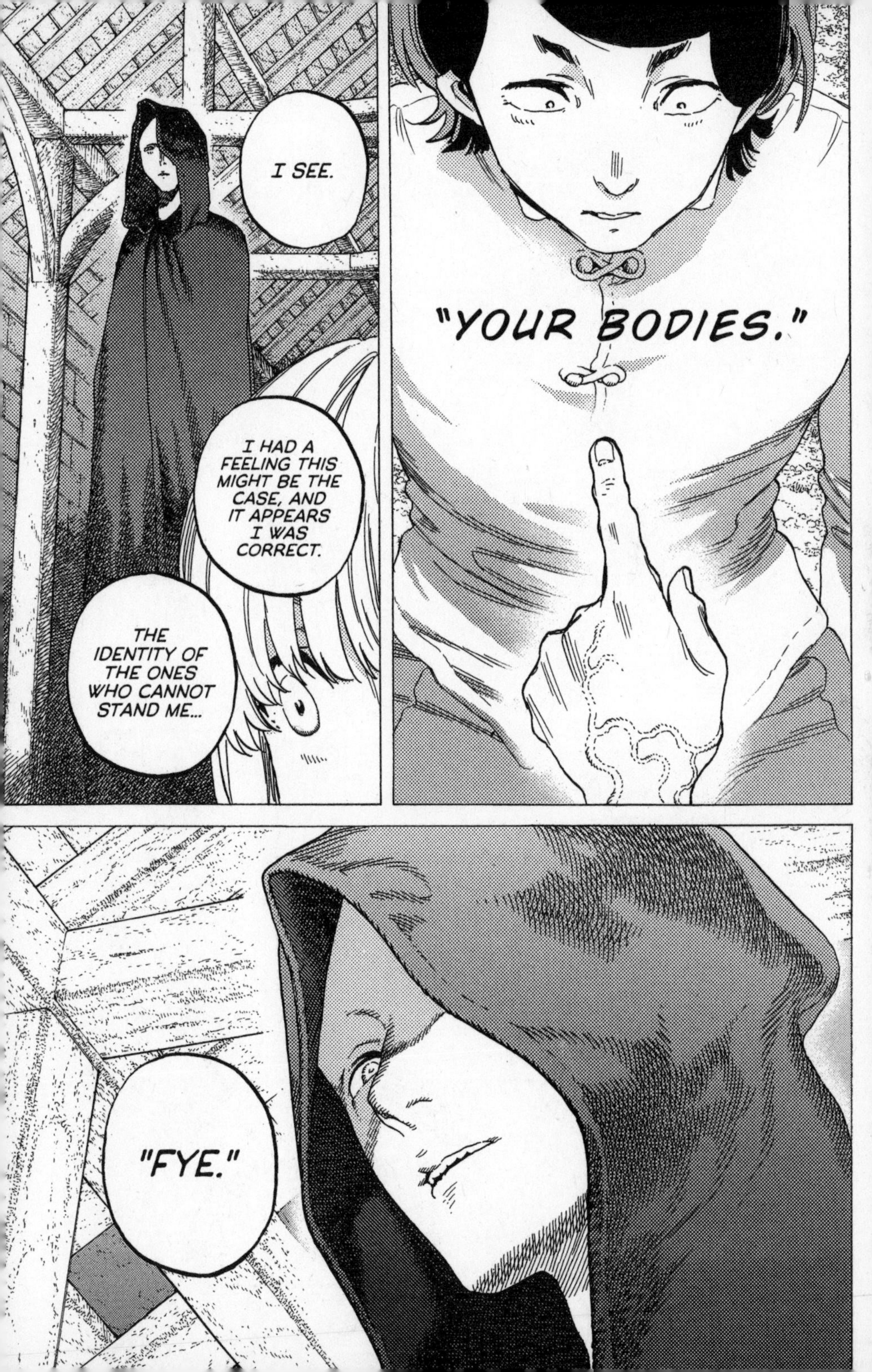

I SEE.
"YOUR BODIES."
I HAD A FEELING THIS MIGHT BE THE CASE, AND IT APPEARS I WAS CORRECT.
THE IDENTITY OF THE ONES WHO CANNOT STAND ME...
"FYE."

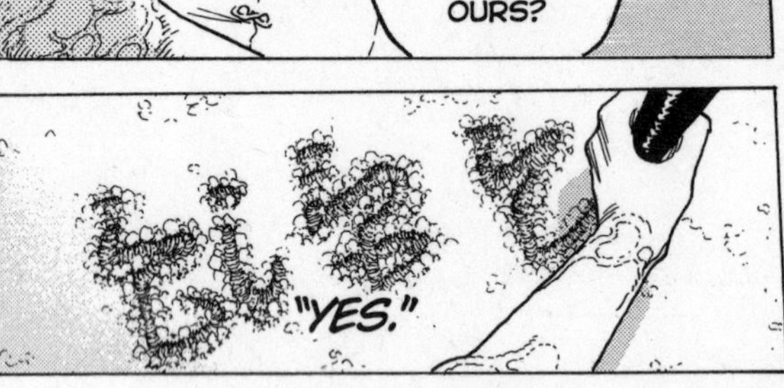

"YOU ARE WRONG."
"WE WISH TO SAVE YOU ALL."

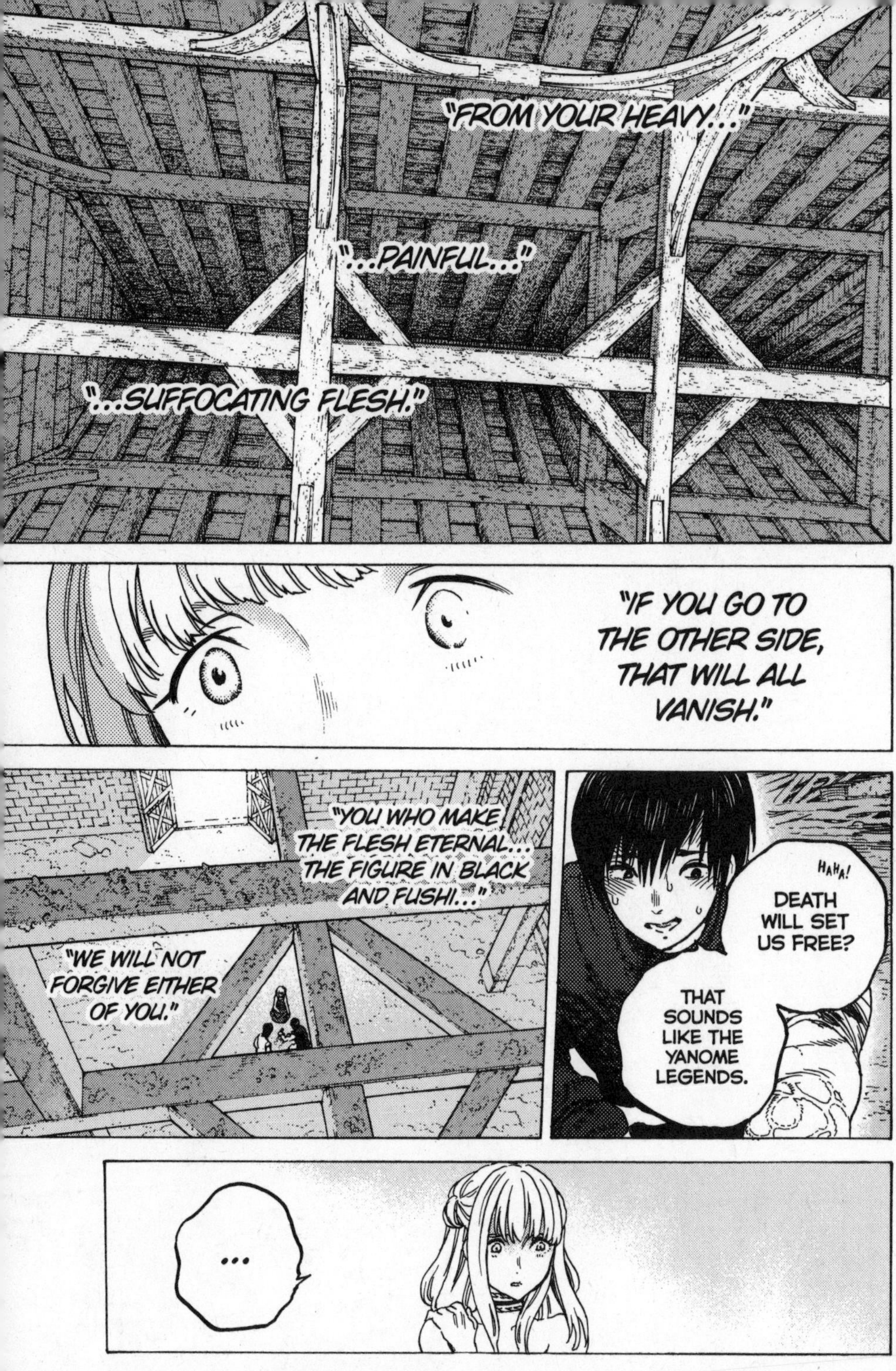

"FROM YOUR HEAVY..."

"...PAINFUL..."

"...SUFFOCATING FLESH."

"IF YOU GO TO THE OTHER SIDE, THAT WILL ALL VANISH."

DEATH WILL SET US FREE?
THAT SOUNDS LIKE THE YANOME LEGENDS.

"YOU WHO MAKE THE FLESH ETERNAL... THE FIGURE IN BLACK AND FUSHI..."
"WE WILL NOT FORGIVE EITHER OF YOU."

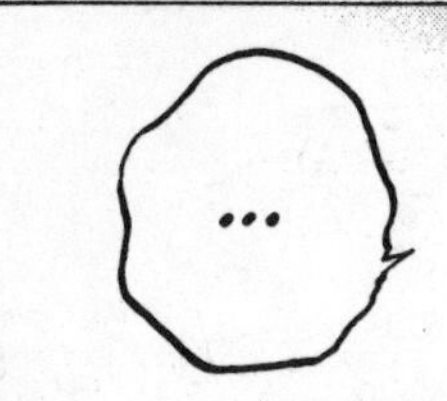

...

HONESTLY, I AM DISAPPOINTED.
ARE YOU PLANNING TO SEND ALL ANIMALS TO THAT WORLD?
YOU HAVE ONLY KILLED AROUND 10,000 SO FAR. WHAT DO YOU THINK YOU CAN DO?
"NUMBERS ARE NOT A PROBLEM."
"SAVING AS MANY OF OUR FRIENDS AS WE POSSIBLY CAN IS OUR GOAL."

ARE YOUR ALLIES WATCHING THIS CONVERSATION?
"THEY MAY BE WATCHING."
TELL ME WHERE THEY'LL ATTACK NEXT.

"THE CHURCH OF BENNETT MAIN TEMPLE."

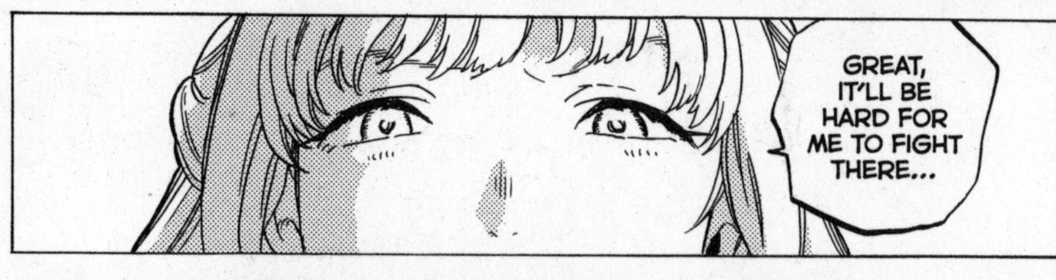
GREAT, IT'LL BE HARD FOR ME TO FIGHT THERE...

THAT'S PROBABLY THEIR PLAN.
THIS IS NO TIME TO TALK ABOUT DISBANDING THE GUARDIANS, KAHAKU. SEND YOUR TROOPS THERE AS QUICKLY AS POSSIBLE.
HUH?
I'M GOING ON AHEAD.
I'LL MEET YOU THERE.

KAHAKU, I STILL NEED YOU.

YOU SHOULD ENJOY ALL THESE CHANGES, TOO!

O-
OKAY!

WUH?!
DID HE ALREADY LEAVE?! HE LEFT HIS HORSEY BEHIND!

YIKESH!
NEIGH
HORSEY—
I HAVE A NEW JOB TO DO.
I MAY HAVE TO LEAVE URALIS AGAIN.

I WILL WAIT FOR YOU HERE IN THE CASTLE, FOR AS MANY YEARS AS IT TAKES...
...BUT PLEASE COME BACK BEFORE CHABO GETS LONELY.
ALL RIGHT.
SO...
...DID YOU GIVE FUSHI HIS REWARD?
NO.
OH? WHY NOT?
YOU DIDN'T LIKE THE WAY HE ANSWERED YOUR QUESTION?
NO, I DID.
SO I'M GOING TO PUT OFF GIVING IT TO HIM FOR A BIT.
?

OH, YEAH.
ABOUT YOUR QUESTION...
"OF COURSE I'D BE HAPPY."
HAVING THESE HEAVY, PAINFUL, SUFFOCATING BODIES...
...IS NOTHING COMPARED TO HOW BAD IT WOULD BE TO NEVER SEE EACH OTHER AGAIN.
...THAT'S PROBABLY WHAT HE'D SAY.

CHWIP
CHWIP
CHWIP
RUSTLE
HOW MUCH FARTHER NORTH?
ANOTHER DAY AND A HALF BY LIGARD.
IS WHAT THAT NOKKER SAID RIGHT?
IT IS CORRECT, BUT IT IS NOT UP TO ME TO DECIDE WHETHER IT IS RIGHT.
IF EVERYONE DIED ACCORD-ING TO THE NOKKERS' SCHEME, WHAT WOULD HAPPEN?
WHO KNOWS? THEY WOULD PROBABLY BE GLAD.
GLAD? THAT'S ALL?
YOU SEEM AWFULLY LIVELY TODAY.
MY DOUBTS ARE GONE.
EVEN IF I GO AWAY, THEY'LL KEEP ATTACKING, RIGHT?
THEY HAVE NO BODIES.
THAT WOULD LIKELY BE ALL.
HEH!

NOW I CAN CRUSH THEM FREELY.

AHHHHH!
AAARGH!

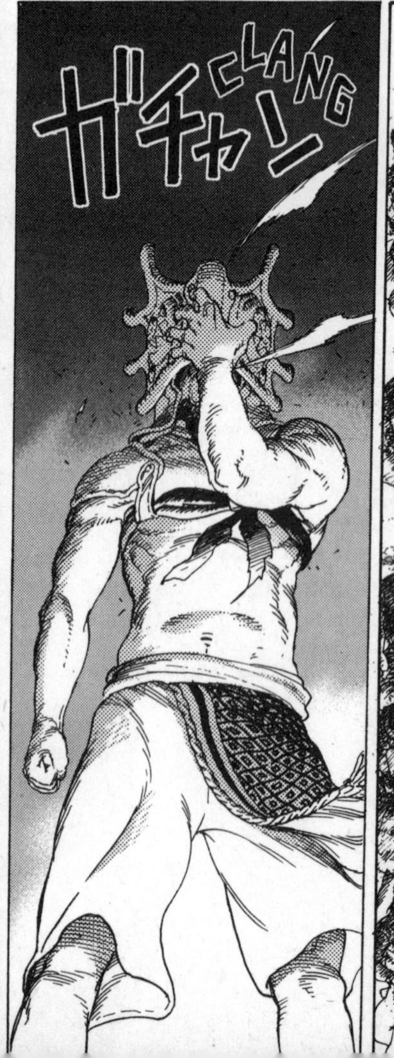
ガチャーン
CLANG

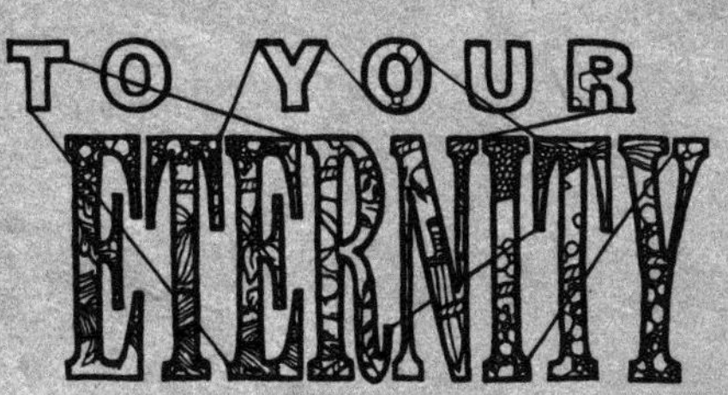
TO YOUR
ETERNITY

#79 The Black Flames of War

EEEEK!

AAAAARGH!

WOW!

I'M SCARED, SIS!
SHHH! STAY HERE UNTIL DAD COMES FOR US!
STAGGER
DAD?!

WE CAN'T STAY HERE ANYMORE!
LET'S RUN FOR IT, SIS!
NO... DAD?!

WHOA!

BA-BANG
BANG
BANG

GET DOWN!

ドサッ
THUD

RUN TOWARD THE WILDERNESS TO THE EAST. THERE ARE NO NOKKERS THERE.

O-OKAY! THANK YOU, SIR!
OH!
WAIT A SECOND!

THAT CUT ON YOUR HAND!

DISINFECT IT WITH THIS AND BANDAGE IT UP.

TOSS

!

YOU A DOCTOR?! WE NEED YOUR HELP, TOO!!

TH-THIS SHOULD EASE THE PAIN A LITTLE...

HANG ON.

THIS IS GOUR, THE OLD PRIEST OF THE CHURCH OF BENNETT.

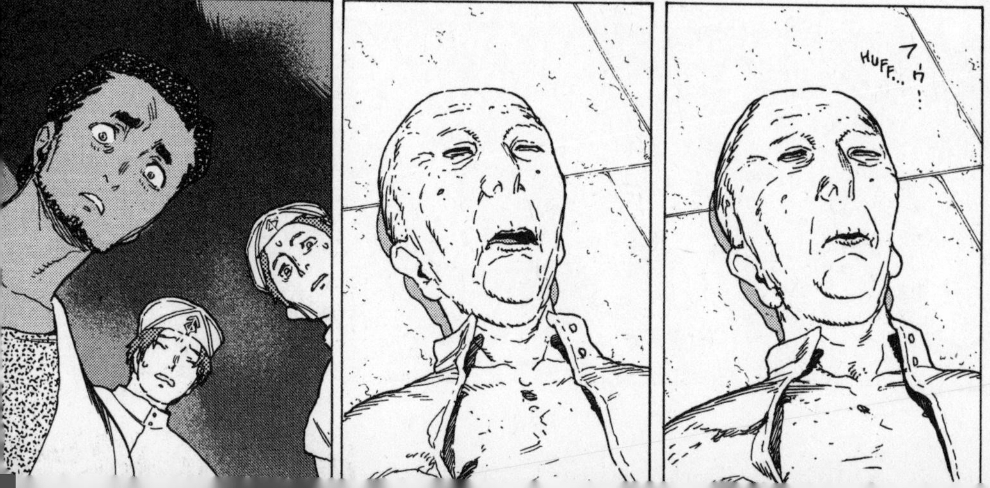

CRASH
!!

HOW MANY PEOPLE ARE LEFT?!
22,000, GATHERED IN THE CENTER OF TOWN.
THE PRIEST IS DEAD. LET'S RUN FOR IT.
Y-YEAH...
THANK YOU, SIR.
BE CAREFUL AND TRY TO GET OUT-SIDE TOWN.

KA-BOOM

...APPARENTLY, EVERYONE BELIEVES GOD WILL SAVE THEM.

THIS CHURCH IS PROTECTED BY THE POWER OF FAITH.

LET US PRAY.

THE NOKKERS ARE ALREADY HERE!!

YOU'LL BE BURIED ALIVE!!

PRIEST GOUR?!

AAAARGH!

RUN FOR IT!

TURN BACK!

WHOA!

CRUNCH

ガラガラガラ
RUMBLE RUMBLE RUMBLE
BANG

RUMBLE
UNDER-
GROUND.
RUMBLE
RUMBLE
GRAB
NO!
AHHH!!
AARGH!!
YARGH!!
THUNK

カハ
COUGH
ピチチ
SHPP
SHRP
ドサッ
THUD
サラ サラ サラ
FLUTTER
FLUTTER
FLUTTER
ビュ!!
WHOOSH!!
ニュル
SHWIP
メリ
CRUNCH
スッ

SNAP
WHUMP
WHUMP
WHUMP
WHUMP
WHUMP
WHAM
WHAM
WHAM
FWUMPH
I'VE GOTTA BOMB UNDER-GROUND!
BWUMP
CLUNK
THERE ARE STILL PEOPLE HERE!!

SHUNK
UGH!
FLUTTER FLUTTER
SHWIP-WIP
SHRP SHRP
THUD
SWHAP
SOMEONE... HELP ME...
!
HANG ON!
WHUMP
CLATTER

WHAP
DAMN IT!
SHWIP
SHK
SHOW YOUR-SELF!!
POW

CLATTER

IT ESCAPED.
BUT THERE ARE 208 OTHERS.

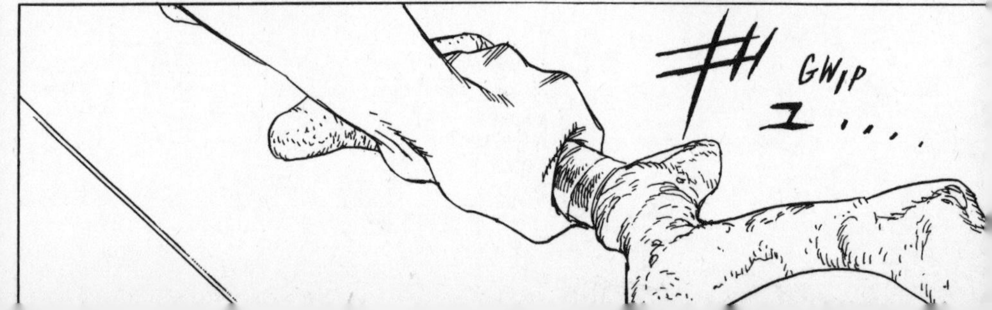
GWIP

BA-BANG
BOOM BOOM

WHERE'S THE ENEMY? WHERE ARE THE NOKKERS?!

YANK

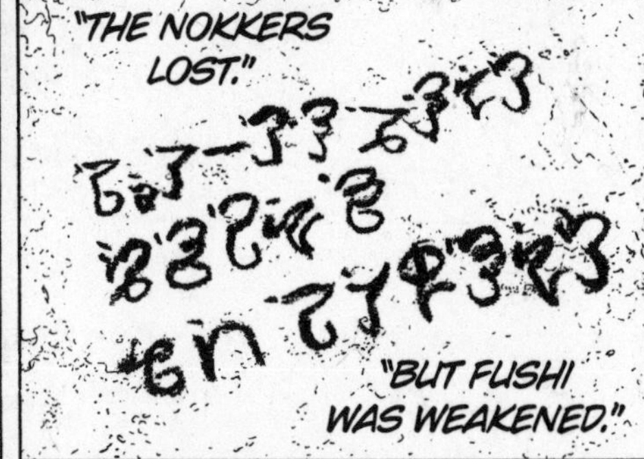
"THE NOKKERS LOST."
"BUT FUSHI WAS WEAKENED."

HUH?

SHK...

"A MESSAGE FROM THEM."

"IF YOU WANT THEM BACK, PLEASE COME TO THE NEXT GAME."

#80 A Tireless Enemy

HEY! YOU THERE! YOU'RE HERETICS, AREN'T YOU?!
YOU'LL SULLY THIS HOLY GROUND!! GET OUT!!

STOP THAT NON-SENSE.

IF YOU WANT TO PROTECT THIS HOLY GROUND, THEN TAKE BACK YOUR RIDICULOUS WORDS.
GH...

MARCH?
I REMEMBER HER.

PARONA?

TONARI?

I REMEMBER HER.

LIGARD?

SO YOU LOST UROY, GUGU, SHIN, PARONA, AND LIGARD, EH?
DID YOU REALLY FORGET THEM?
SCRUFF
SCRUFF
I CAN'T REMEMBER.

YOU WROTE THIS YOURSELF SO YOU WOULDN'T FORGET, RIGHT?
YEAH, BUT IT DIDN'T WORK.
I CAN'T PICTURE THEM CLEARLY, EVEN WITH THAT PAPER.
LOSING THE FIRE-BREATHING MAN IS A HUGE BLOW.
OUR OPPONENT'S NUMBERS ARE UNLIMITED.
IF THEY TOOK FIVE FORMS IN ONE BATTLE, CAN YOU REALLY LAST AGAINST THEM?

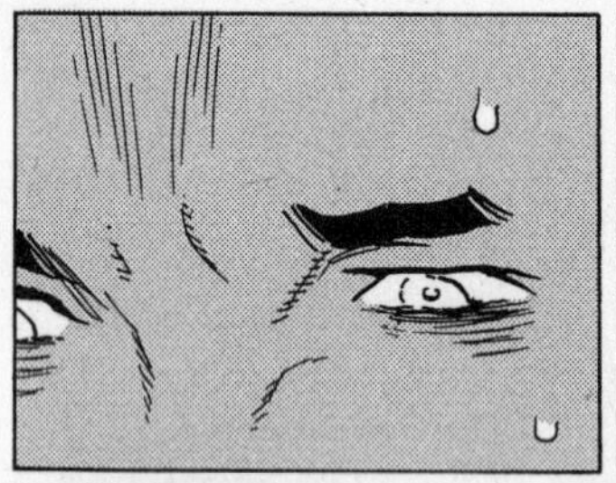

TO SAVE MANY LIVES DEMANDS SOME SACRIFICE.

AT TIMES LIKE THESE...
...WHAT AM I SUPPOSED TO SAY TO THEM?

BE HAPPY ON THE OTHER SIDE...

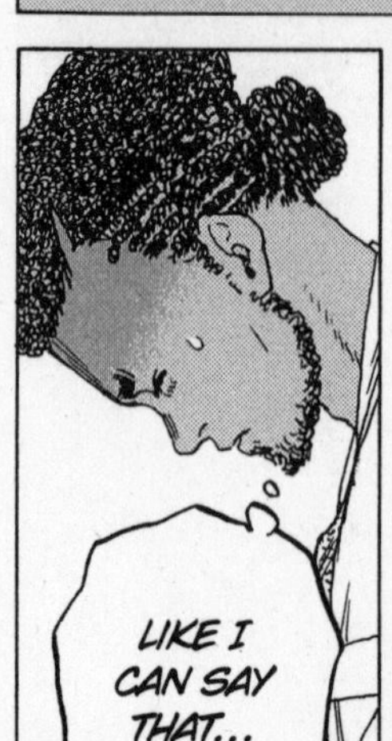
LIKE I CAN SAY THAT...

I AM SURE THEY'LL BE EVEN HAPPIER ON THE OTHER SIDE THAN THEY WERE HERE.

I'M SORRY...

DAMN IT!
DAMN IT!

HELLO THERE.
...WERE YOU FAMILY?

OH...
YOU'RE THE ONE WHO WAS OUTSIDE...
...COME TO THINK OF IT, AFTER I SPOKE TO YOU, A LOT OF PEOPLE LEFT THE CHURCH.

...NO.
I'M ALONE.
...OH, YOU ARE?

NO, I DIDN'T DO ANYTHING...
...

YOU HELPED, DIDN'T YOU?
THANKS.

IF WE CAN OBTAIN HAPPINESS BY DYING...
...THEN WHAT ARE WE LIVING FOR?

...TO LEARN JUST THAT.

OH, THAT'S ONLY MY PERSONAL OPINION THAT JUST POPPED UP.
THERE MIGHT BE A BETTER ANSWER TO THAT QUESTION.
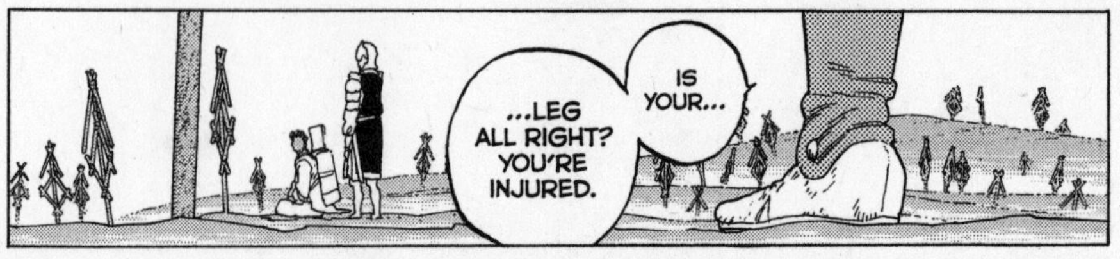
IS YOUR...
...LEG ALL RIGHT? YOU'RE INJURED.

TAKE THESE.

YOU DIDN'T NOTICE?
COME HERE, JOAAN. WE NEED TO TALK.

YEAH.

GOOD FORTUNE TO YOU.

TAKE A LOOK AT THIS.
Fwlp

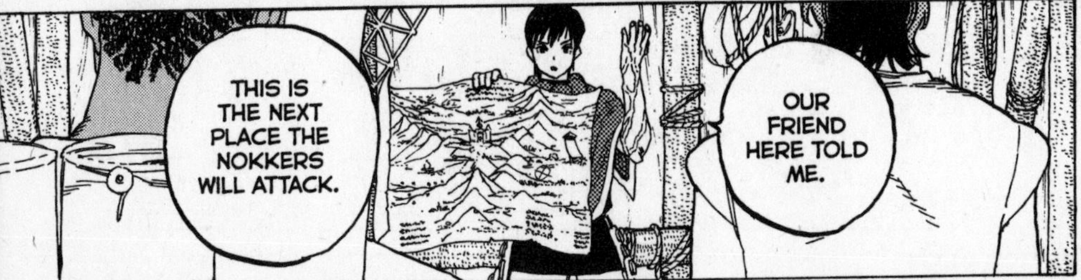
OUR FRIEND HERE TOLD ME.
THIS IS THE NEXT PLACE THE NOKKERS WILL ATTACK.

"IF YOU WANT THEM BACK, PLEASE COME TO THE NEXT GAME."

HEY!
WHUMP
YOU HANDLE THINGS HERE!
I'LL FOLLOW HIM!
H-HANG ON A SECOND!
WAIT!
IT'S TOO DANGER-OUS TO GO ALONE!
TMP
TMP

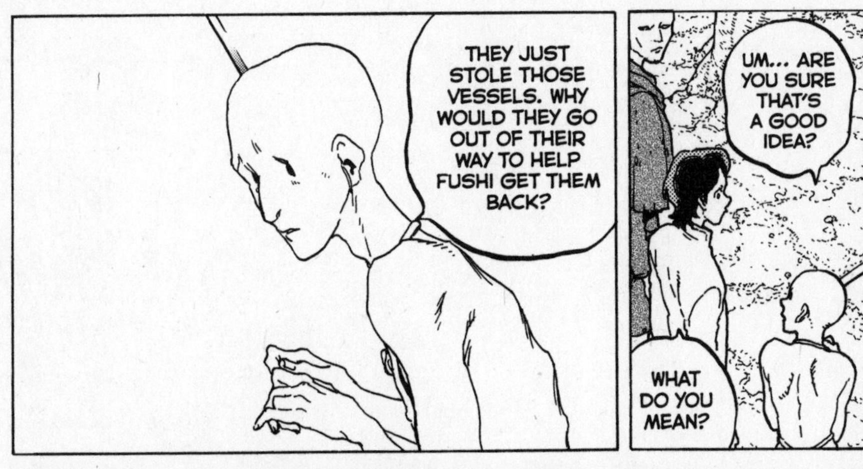
UM... ARE YOU SURE THAT'S A GOOD IDEA?
WHAT DO YOU MEAN?
THEY JUST STOLE THOSE VESSELS. WHY WOULD THEY GO OUT OF THEIR WAY TO HELP FUSHI GET THEM BACK?

HUH?
IF IT WERE ME, I'D JUST STAY HIDDEN UNDER-GROUND.

WHOOOOOOOOSH

IS THIS THE RIGHT PLACE?
YES.

SPLORCH
ドッ
!
SHRK
UH-OH, I CAN'T GO ANY FARTHER.
SCHLUP
SPLAT
I'LL GO OVER IT.
I SHOULD'VE OBTAINED A PIGEON IN TOWN.
ゴポッ
GLOPP
THEY'RE HERE.
CHOOM

SPLASH
CRACK!
TUMP

UNDER THERE, EH?!
SHWIP

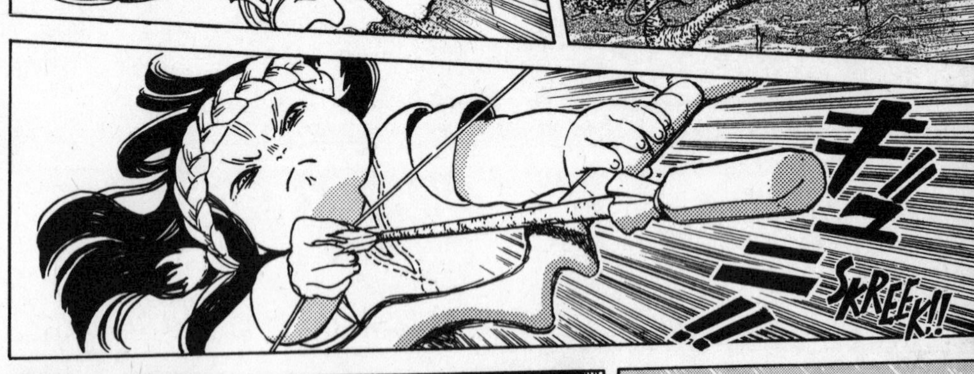

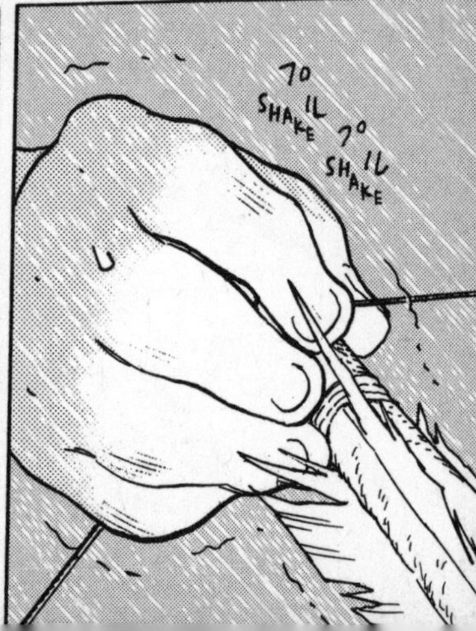

WHAP!!
バチン!!
SPLORCH
!
VWHIRRL
SPLAP!!
UGH!

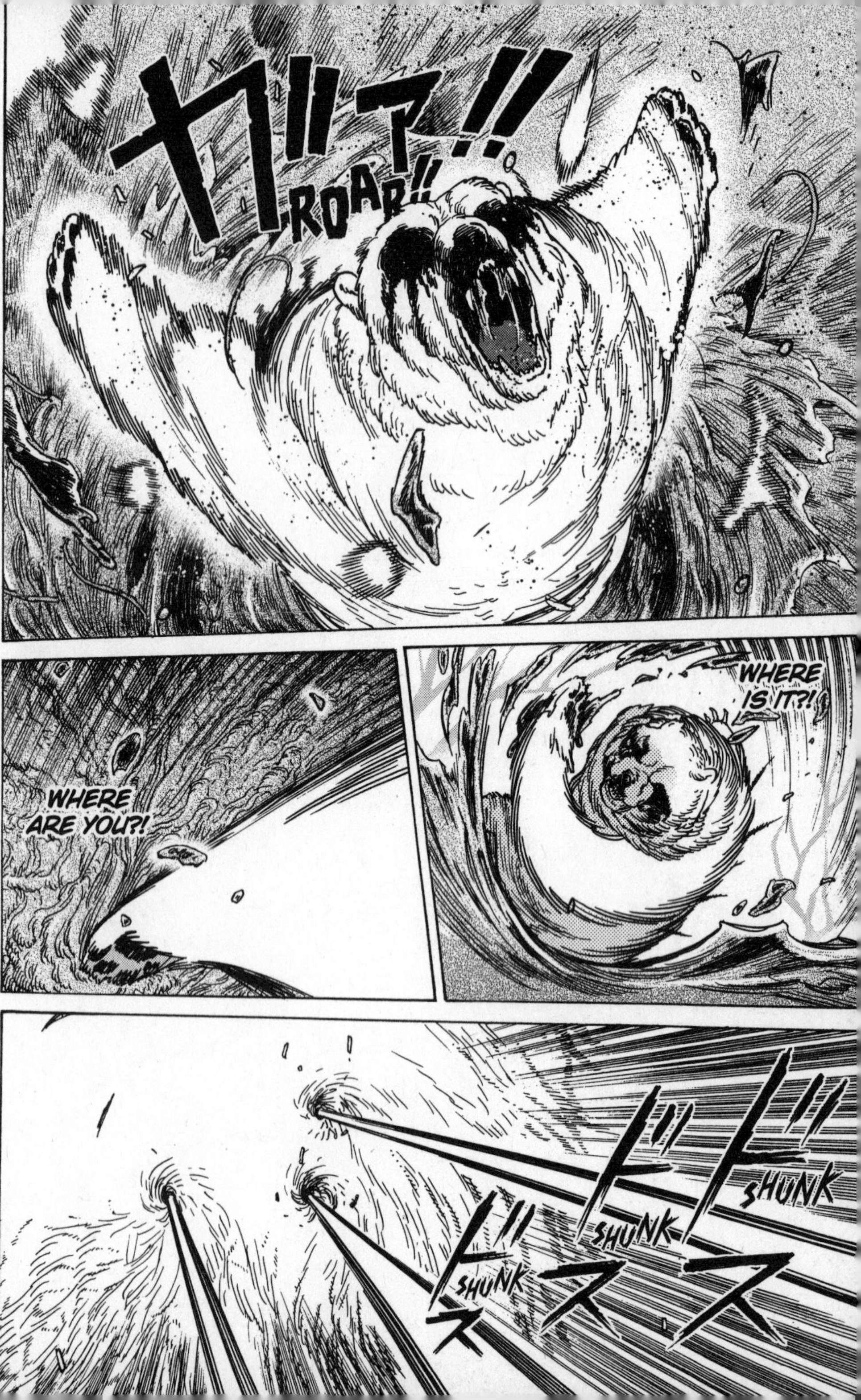

ROAR!!

WHUMP
I DON'T THINK SO!!
WHAP
THOKK!
SCHLORP
DAMN IT!
I CAN'T MOVE!!

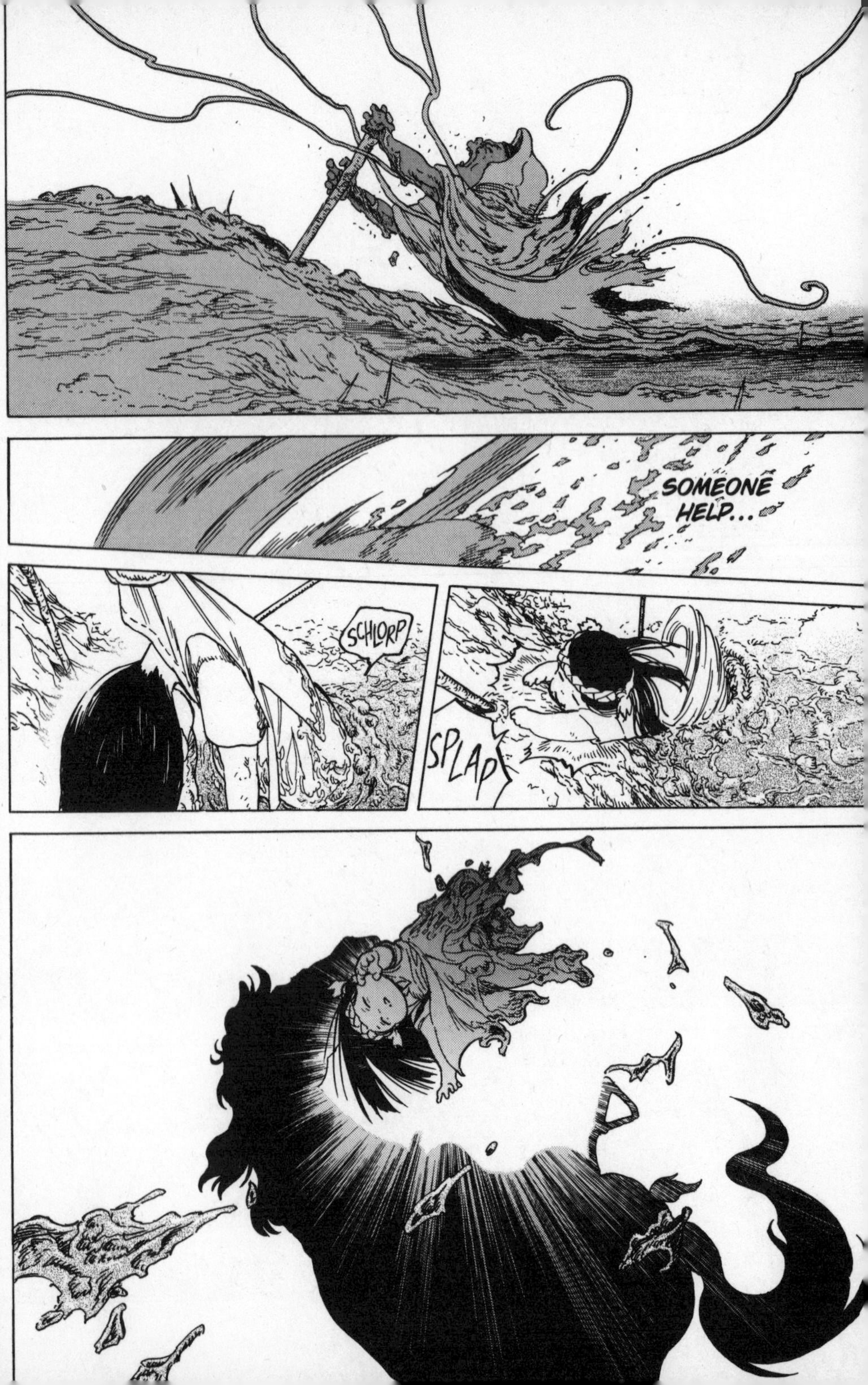

SOMEONE HELP...
SCHLORP
SPLAP

WHUMPH!
THUD!
WH-
WHAT JUST
HAPPENED?!

#81 Spreading Consciousness
CLOP
CLOP
CLOP
WHAM
WHAM
!
ZOOM

WHAP
SLASH
NEIGH
WHUMPH!
RUSTLE
WHAM!

YEOW...

ISN'T THIS... THE HORSE I GOT BACK IN URALIS?
WHAT'S IT DOING HERE? DON'T TELL ME IT CAME TO MY RESCUE?

WHUMP
WHOA!!

THAT IS A HORSE MADE FROM YOUR FLESH.
IT HAS NO ABILITY TO ACQUIRE AS YOU DO, BUT IT IS EXTREMELY RESISTANT TO DAMAGE.

DID YOU MAKE IT?!
I PREPARED IT SOME TIME AGO, BUT I WISHED TO GIVE IT TO YOU WHEN YOU HAD NEED OF IT.

WHY?
A HORSE ISN'T GONNA–

UH-OH! THAT NOKKER'S STILL ALIVE!
I'VE GOTTA FINISH IT OFF THIS TIME!!

CHOMP

WHUMPH

WHAM

YEOW!
WHAT'RE YOU DOING?!

ARE YOU TELLING ME NOT TO GO?!

NO, THAT'S RIDICU-LOUS.

WHAM!
YIPE!

WOOF!!
IF YOU DON'T SETTLE DOWN, I'M NOT GONNA LOOK AFTER YOU!!

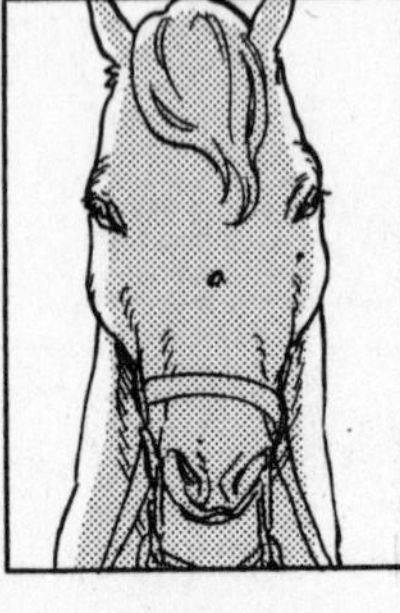

...

BUT WHAT ELSE CAN I...

YOU'RE RIGHT. I DON'T HAVE A CHANCE AGAINST IT RIGHT NOW.
I KNOW I'M JUST GONNA GET BEAT IF I WALK BACK IN THERE.

THAT MUCK IN THE SWAMP GETS IN THE WAY, SO I CAN'T EVEN ATTACK PROPERLY

IT HAPPENED THEN, TOO.

A WALL OF PEOPLE BLOCKED MY WAY...
...AND WHILE I WAS DISTRACTED, IT STABBED ME EASILY.

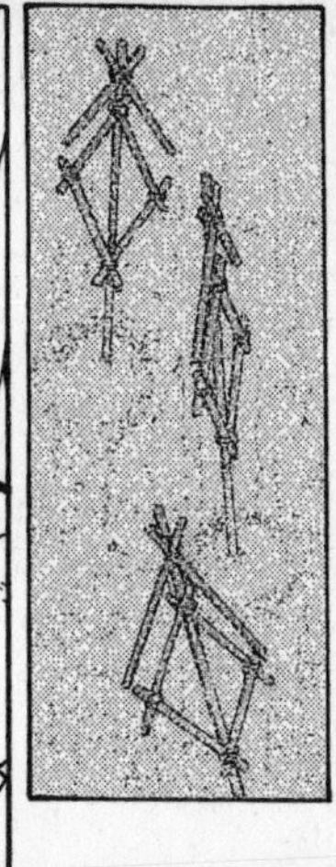

OH, YEAH...
COME TO THINK OF IT, NO NOKKERS ATTACKED WHILE I WAS TRAPPED IN METAL.

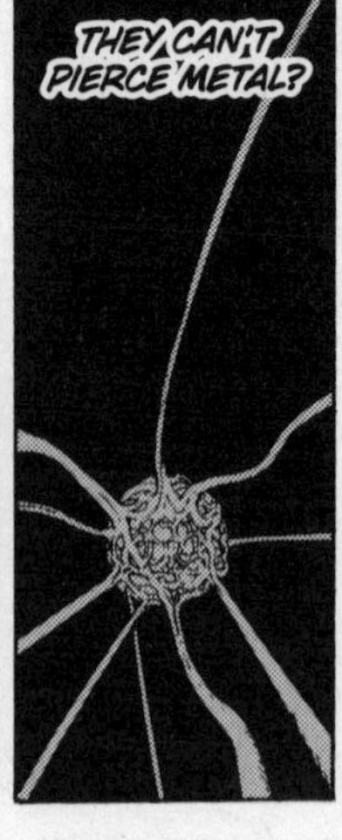
THEY CAN'T PIERCE METAL?

SHWIP
ARMOR WOULD PROBABLY BE BETTER...
...BUT I MIGHT ALSO BE ABLE TO BLOCK NOKKER ATTACKS WITH WEAPONS, LIKE I DID BACK ON JANANDA...

BUT THESE WEIGH ME DOWN AND MAKE IT HARD TO MOVE.
I WISH I COULD ATTACK FROM A DISTANCE, BUT THE EXPLODING ARROWS DON'T WORK ON NOKKERS IN THE SWAMP.

IF ONLY I COULD SENSE WHERE THEY'RE HIDING ON MY OWN...
...

GUY IN BLACK.
DO I HAVE ANY POWER THAT WOULD LET ME SENSE WHERE NOKKERS ARE, LIKE YOU?

IT IS POSSIBLE.
BUT YOU WILL HAVE TO EXPAND YOUR SENSORY CORTEX.

...WHAT'S THAT?
I SHALL SHOW YOU.
CLOSE YOUR EYES.

SNAP

I JUST SEVERED PART OF YOU.
TELL ME WHERE IT WAS.

HUH? IT DIDN'T HURT...
IF YOU CONCENTRATE, YOU SHOULD BE ABLE TO TELL WHAT IS MISSING.
CONCENTRATE...

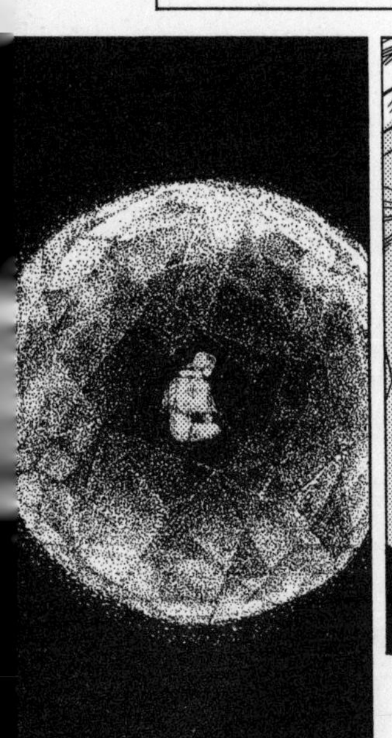

THE END OF THAT ROPE?

S-S-SO...
...IF I LEARNED TO MAKE BIG SHIPS...
...AS LONG AS I'M CONNECTED TO IT, I COULD SENSE ANYTHING TOUCHING ONE OF THOSE SHIPS?!

IF YOU COULD CREATE LAND FROM THE END OF THIS ROPE...
...THAT LAND WOULD BE 100% YOUR TERRITORY.

THAT IS RIGHT.
AND WITH PROPER TRAINING, YOUR SENSES SHOULD BECOME SHARPER.

IF I CAN LEARN TO MAKE THAT SWAMP...

BUT IT'S HARD TO GRASP THE SENSATION OF THIS MUCK...

I CAN MAKE ROCKS AND TREES FOR NOW...

BUT WHAT'S THE NEXT STEP AFTER THAT? NOKKERS IN THE MUCK ARE INVINCIBLE...

WHAP!!

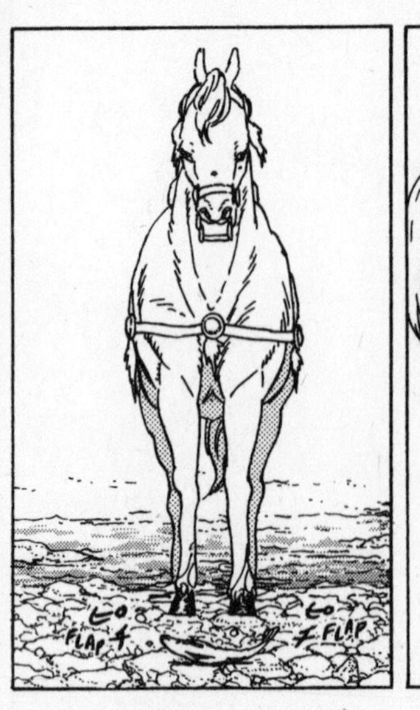
FLAP
FLAP

SHORT
WHAT? DID YOU CATCH THIS?

SORRY, BUT I DON'T REALLY LIKE FISH.

WHAP

HEY! I SAID I DON'T WANT ANY...

HAHA, WOW.
SO YOU'RE GOOD AT CATCHING FISH?
YOU'RE ALMOST LIKE...
...ALMOST LIKE...
...

HEY, YEAH.
THAT MIGHT WORK...

THANKS, HORSE!

COME ON OUT, NOKKER!
I CAME BACK! COME STEAL ME!
SHOOM
BAM
SO THAT'S WHERE YOU ARE?
I'LL SCOOP YOU RIGHT OUTTA THERE.
GLORP

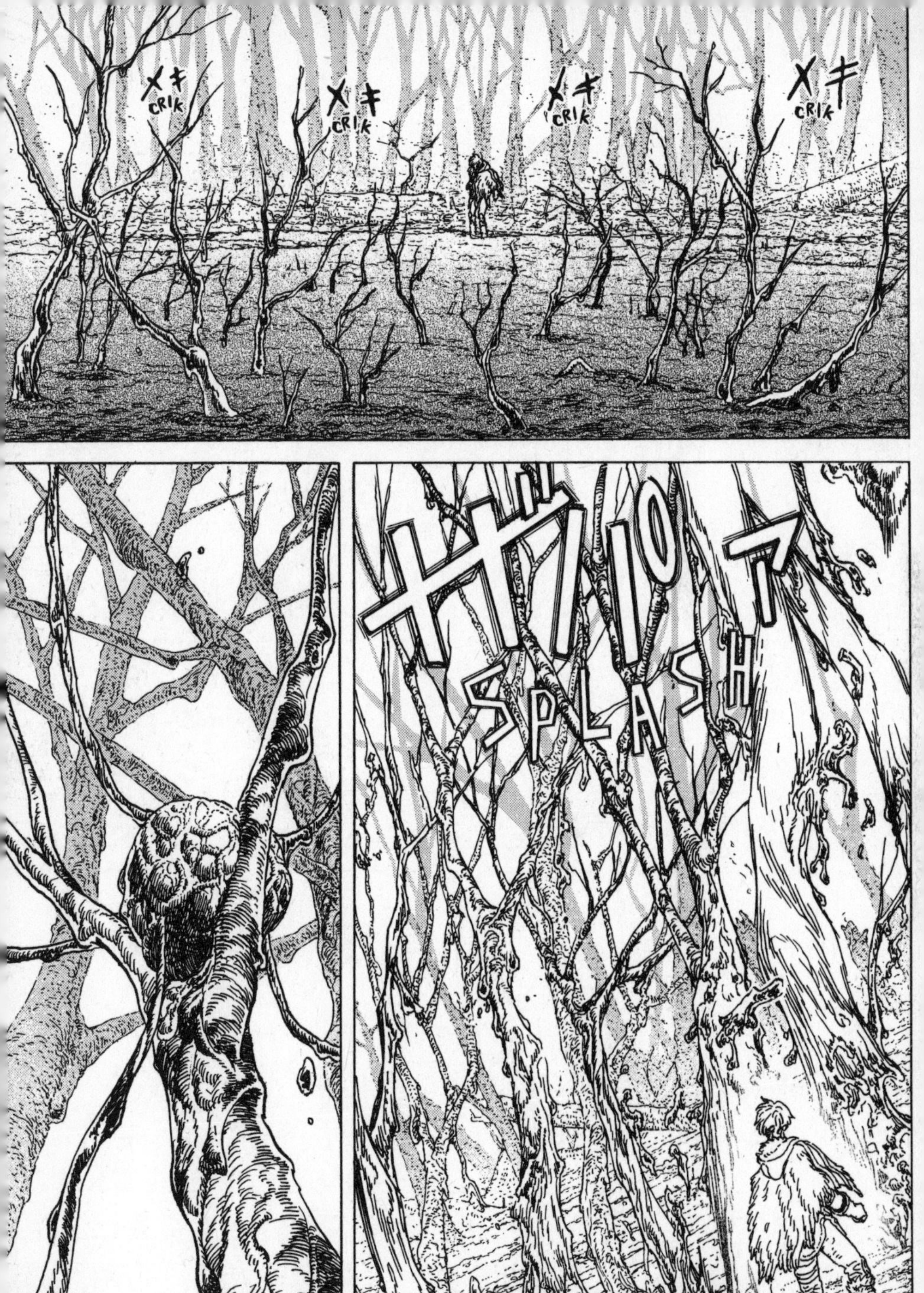
メキ
CRIK
メキ
CRIK
メキ
CRIK
メキ
CRIK
ギパァ
SPLASH

SHUNK

TSSSS

ALL RIGHT.

I DID IT...

PIORAN.

#82 Bet on the Future

ONCE YOU ARE ABLE TO MAKE LARGER OBJECTS...
...YOUR PERCEPTION WILL EXPAND ACCORD-INGLY.
BWUMP

BWUMP
BWUMP
BWUMP
BWUMP

ROUGHLY 30 METERS, HUH?

FUSHI! ARE YOU ALL RIGHT?!

I BROUGHT ARMOR.

YEAH. IT GOT ME ONCE, BUT I GOT THEM BACK.

THANKS TO THIS HORSE.

TH-THANK GOODNESS.

THEN YOU GOT ALL YOUR MEMORIES BACK, TOO, RIGHT?!

"I'M SORRY. THEY TRICKED ME AS WELL."

YEAH, SURE.

IT'S EASY TO MAKE UP EXCUSES.

AREN'T YOU GLAD YOU CAME HERE AND LEARNED WHAT POWER YOU NEED, FUSHI?
IT IS A POWER YOU NEED TO GAIN BEFORE FIGHTING THE NOKKER BURIED UNDER-GROUND, 131 KM AWAY.

YEAH, TRUSTING THAT NOKKER IS GOING TO BE INCREDIBLY HARD.
MISTER BLACK DIDN'T TELL YOU ANYTHING?

APPAR-ENTLY, HE KNEW AND INTENTION-ALLY DIDN'T TELL ME.
LIKE ALWAYS.

SKRITCH
SKRITCH

"THE NEXT NOKKER ATTACK WILL APPARENTLY BE ON THE FOOTHILL TOWN OF BISSEIGH."

I'M ON MY WAY!
FUSHI!

CHOMP
WHAP
THUD
DON'T BE HASTY, FUSHI. I'LL SEND SOME TROOPS FROM URALIS.
THEY'LL NEVER MAKE IT IN TIME!
IT'S A TOWN! THERE ARE PEOPLE THERE!
I'M SAYING THIS BECAUSE IT'S A TOWN!
HOW MANY VESSELS DO YOU PLAN TO LOSE IN THE NEXT BATTLE?
I-I DON'T PLAN TO LOSE ANY!
THEN WAIT HERE!
DON'T BE STUPID! ARE YOU TELLING ME NOT TO DO ANYTHING?!
THAT'S NOT WHAT I'M SAYING.
WAIT UNTIL YOU'RE STRONG ENOUGH TO DEFEND YOURSELF BEFORE YOU GO INTO BATTLE!
ARE YOU PLANNING TO HAVE ONE PERSON STOLEN EVERY TIME YOU SAVE ANOTHER?!

ARE YOU TELLING ME TO IGNORE PEOPLE DYING JUST TO SAVE MY INFINITE LIFE?!

WHAT GIVES YOU THE RIGHT TO LIMIT ME LIKE THAT?!

THE PEOPLE YOU FORGOT ARE YELLING FOR ME TO STOP YOU!!

...

HUH?

THERE'S A NOKKER COMING!
!
YOU CAN DO THIS, CAN'T YOU, LEFT HAND?
GET BACK, YOU TWO!
I SHALL FIGHT!
HEY, ARE YOU SERIOUS, KAHAKU?!
SHOOM
WIN THIS FIGHT AND REGAIN THEIR TRUST!!
WHOOSH
WHOOSH

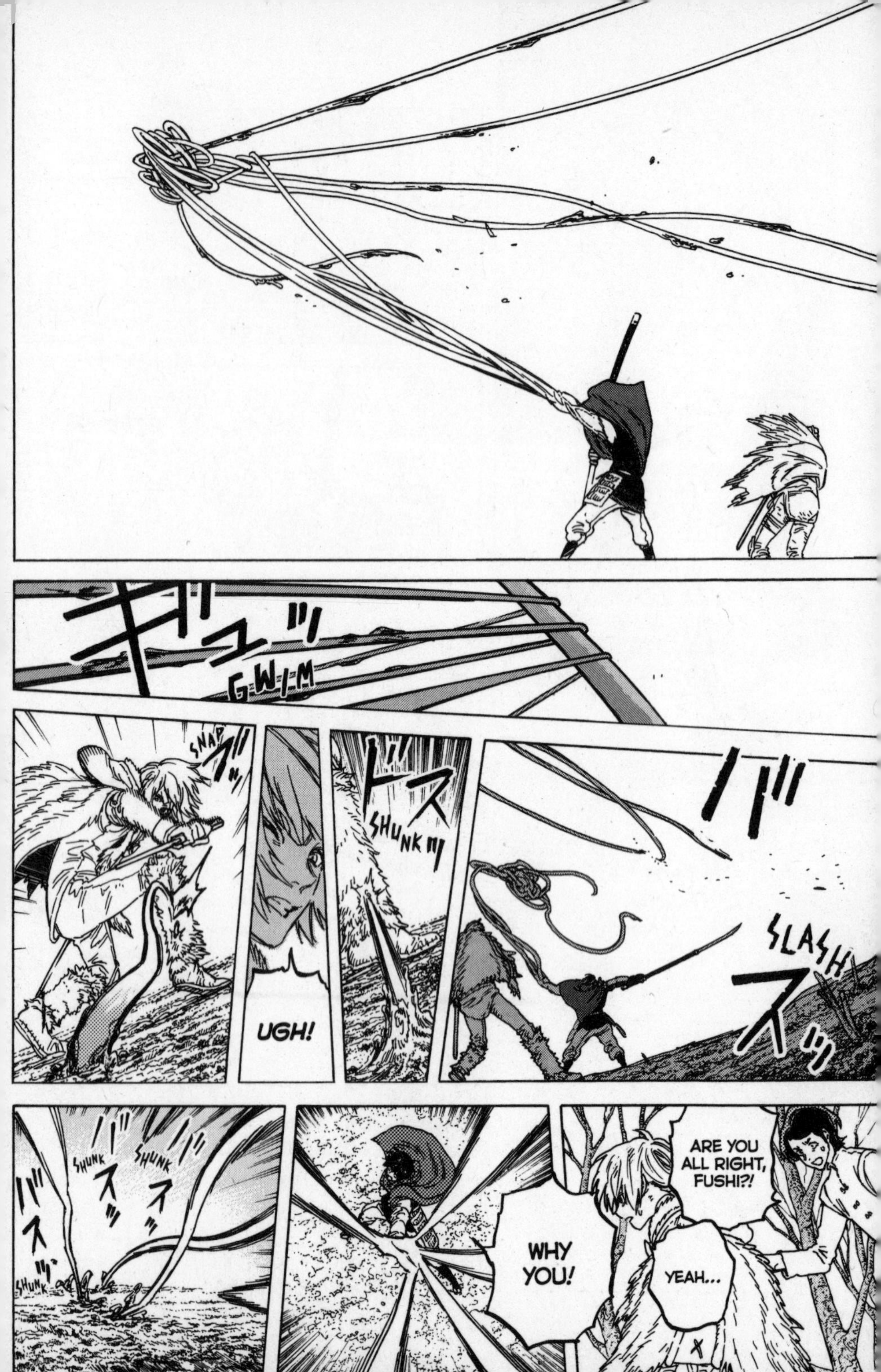
GWIM
SNAP
UGH!
SHUNK
SLASH
SHUNK
SHUNK
SHUNK
ARE YOU ALL RIGHT, FUSHI?!
YEAH...
WHY YOU!

POP

SQUEEZE

SPLASH

PLOP
YOU DID IT! THAT WAS AMAZING, KAHAKU!
N-NOT BAD!!

YES...

ハァ HUFF

ハァ HUFF

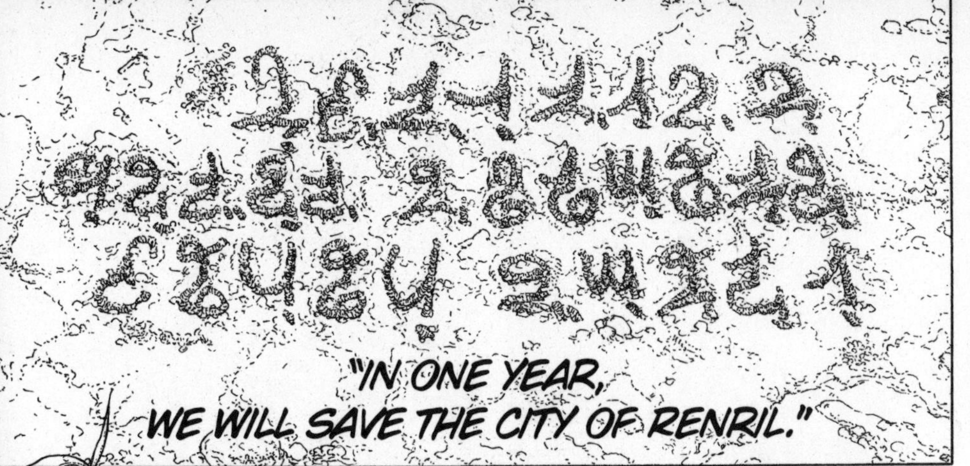
"IN ONE YEAR,
WE WILL SAVE THE CITY OF RENRIL."

"WE INVITE YOU TO JOIN US."

"IF YOU DO NOT COME...
...WE WILL KILL KAHAKU AND THIS TRAITOR."

...
RENRIL IS THE BIGGEST CITY ON THE CONTINENT.
IF THEY ATTACK THERE, THEY COULD EASILY KILL 100,000 PEOPLE.

WE AREN'T VERY STRONG, AND WE DIE QUICKLY...
WHEN WILL THIS BATTLE END?
PROBABLY NEVER.
OR IF IT DOES, IT WON'T BE UNTIL AFTER WE'RE ALL DEAD.

FUSHI, AS LONG AS YOU'RE WELL, YOU CAN FIGHT IT.
DON'T LET IT STEAL THE PEOPLE...
...WHO RISKED THEIR LIVES FOR YOU.
DON'T FORGET THEM.

LET'S FORMULATE A PLAN.
FUSHI, WHAT IS YOUR HOMEWORK?

...
ALL RIGHT...

...LEARNING TO MAKE BIGGER THINGS.
IF I CAN DO THAT, I'LL HAVE THE ADVANTAGE IN BATTLE.
OH, YES, YOU WISH TO LEARN TO MAKE LARGE BOATS, RIGHT?

I CAN HAVE PAPA PREPARE WHATEVER WE NEED.
LEARN TO MAKE THEM IN THREE MONTHS.

THREE MONTHS...

YEAH, JUST FOCUS ON GETTING STRONGER FOR THREE MONTHS.
LEAVE EVERYTHING ELSE TO ME DURING THAT TIME.
FIGHTING NOKKERS, THE EVAC-UATION OF RENRIL, ALL OF IT...

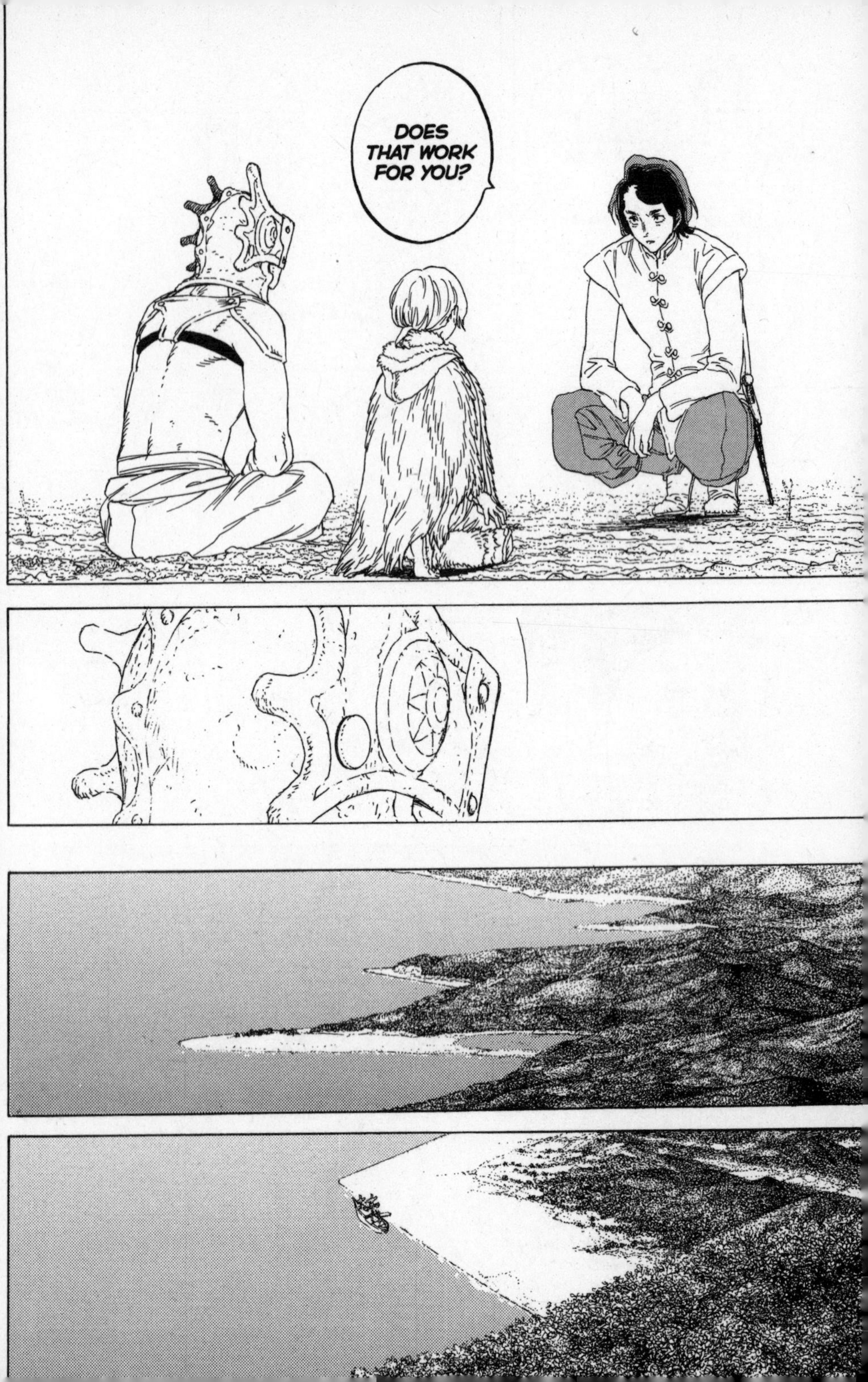

DOES THAT WORK FOR YOU?

THIS WAY, FUSHI.
THERE'S NOTHING AROUND HERE.
NO TOWNS OR PEOPLE.
CLOP
JUST YOUR NEW BASE.

THERE WERE PLANS TO BUILD A CITY HERE YEARS AGO, BUT THOSE FELL THROUGH...
...SO THEY JUST LEFT THIS HERE.
THERE ARE OLD GOODS STILL INSIDE, SO FEEL FREE TO USE THEM.
...

C-CAN I REALLY USE THAT BOAT?!
YEAH.
IF ANYTHING HAPPENS, RELEASE A MESSENGER BIRD. IT'LL FLY TO URALIS.

THANK YOU. FOR EVERY-THING.
I'LL DO MY BEST!

YEAH...

FUSHI, I'LL HEAD TEMPO-RARILY TO URALIS AS WELL.
I WILL RETURN, SO DO YOUR BEST UNTIL THEN.

DON'T YOU DIE EITHER, KAHAKU.

O-OKAY!

SEE YOU LATER.

WOW!
ピュギー
SQUEAL
WHOA!
THE ANIMALS THAT WERE ON THE BOAT ARE STILL ALIVE?

LET'S DO OUR BEST TOGETHER.

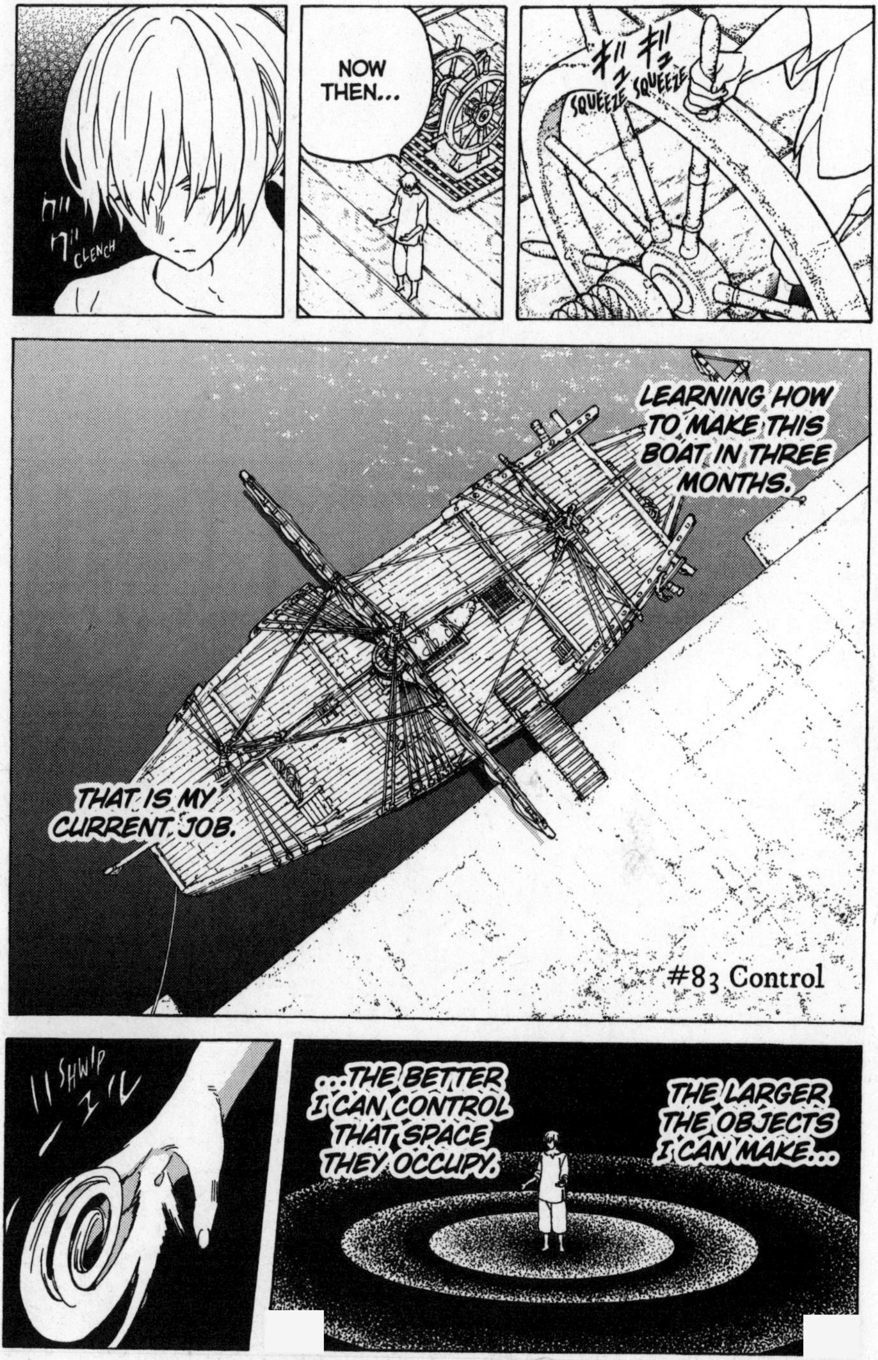

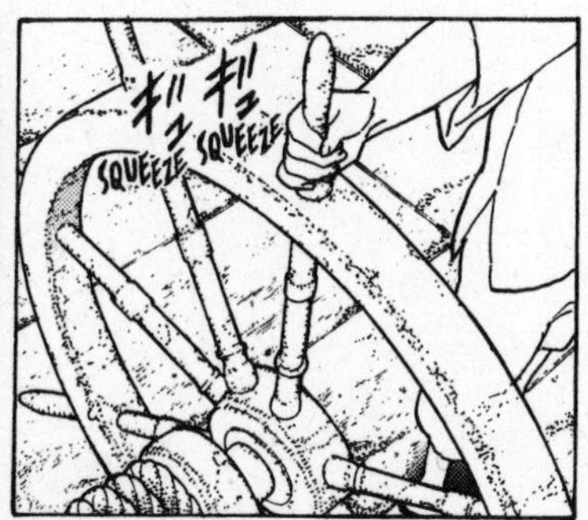

LEARNING HOW TO MAKE THIS BOAT IN THREE MONTHS.

THAT IS MY CURRENT JOB.

#83 Control

THE LARGER THE OBJECTS I CAN MAKE...
...THE BETTER I CAN CONTROL THAT SPACE THEY OCCUPY.

SHWIP

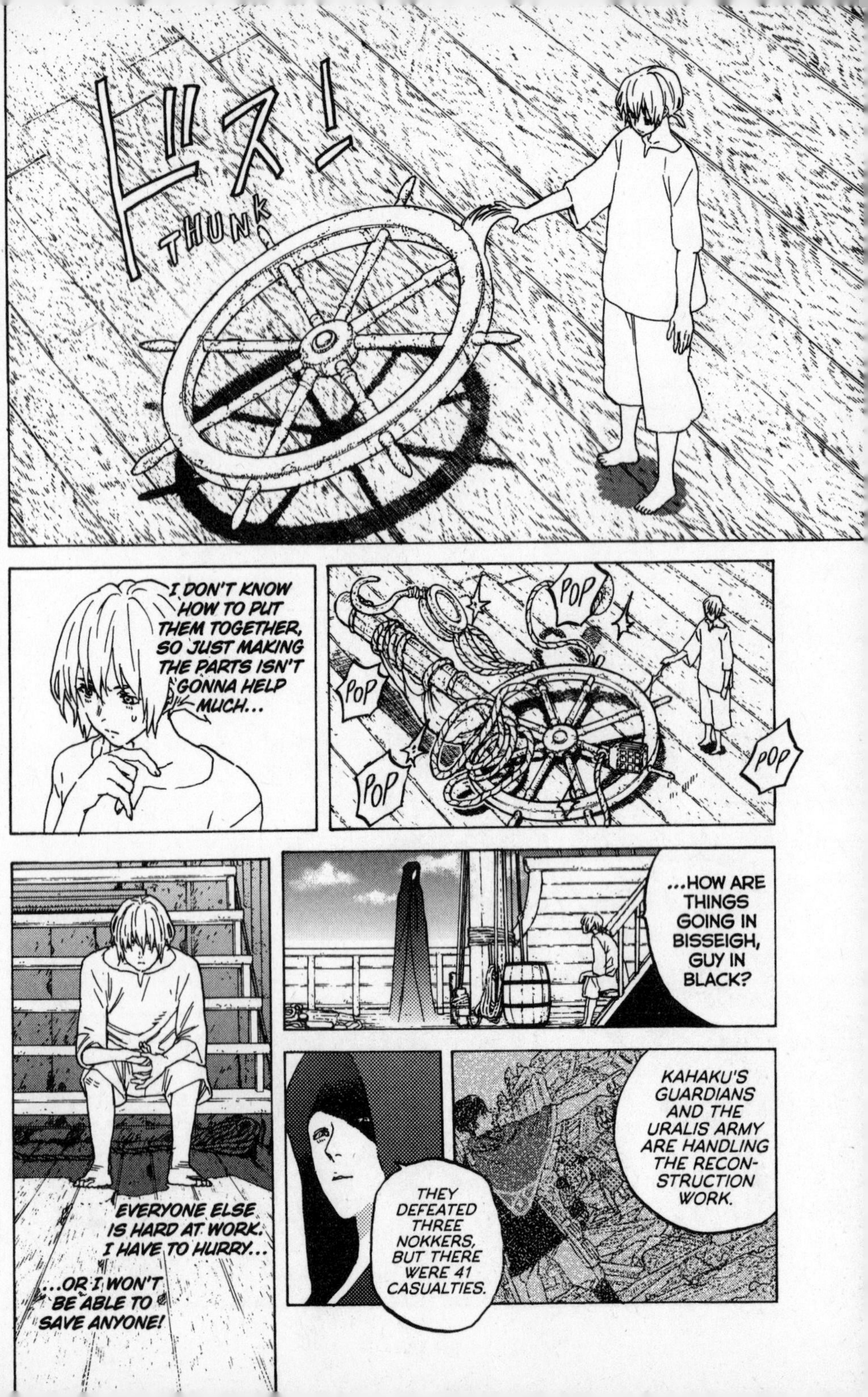

ドスン
THUNK

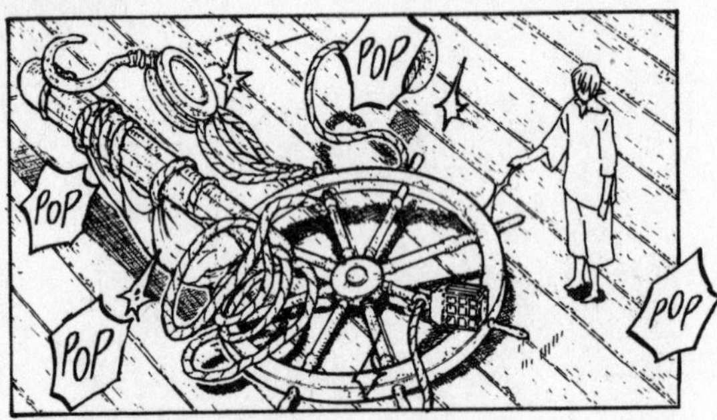
POP
POP
POP
POP

I DON'T KNOW HOW TO PUT THEM TOGETHER, SO JUST MAKING THE PARTS ISN'T GONNA HELP MUCH...

...HOW ARE THINGS GOING IN BISSEIGH, GUY IN BLACK?

KAHAKU'S GUARDIANS AND THE URALIS ARMY ARE HANDLING THE RECON-STRUCTION WORK.
THEY DEFEATED THREE NOKKERS, BUT THERE WERE 41 CASUALTIES.

EVERYONE ELSE IS HARD AT WORK. I HAVE TO HURRY...
...OR I WON'T BE ABLE TO SAVE ANYONE!

ROYAL CAPITAL, RENRIL

Y-YOU WANT US TO ACCEPT YOUR PROTECTION?

YES...

...PRINCESS.

HOW WAS THIS PREDICTION OF A NOKKER ATTACK ON RENRIL DISCOVERED?

I AM ACQUAINTED WITH SOME-ONE WHO CAN COMMUNICATE WITH THEM.

AND WHY DID YOU NOT BRING THEM WITH YOU?

DESPITE HIS VALUE, HE HAS BEEN DECLARED A HERETIC BY THE CHURCH OF BENNETT... I THOUGHT IT PRUDENT TO BE CAREFUL.

WHY WOULD THE NOKKERS GO OUT OF THEIR WAY TO INFORM YOU OF THEIR PLANS WHEN A SURPRISE ATTACK WOULD CLEARLY BE MORE ADVANTAGEOUS?

...

I DO NOT UNDER-STAND IT MYSELF.

I CAN ONLY ASSUME THEY ARE ENJOYING US HUMANS TAKING A MORE ACTIVE ROLE IN THIS WAR...

YOU SPEAK AS IF IT WERE SOME SORT OF GAME...

...WHAT EXACTLY IS IT YOU WOULD LIKE US TO DO?

THE CITY WILL BECOME A BATTLE-FIELD.

I WOULD ASK THAT YOU EVACUATE THE PEOPLE WITHIN THE CITY AND CASTLE.

THE URALIS ARMY WILL THEN ELIMINATE THE NOKKERS.

HEH!
YOU WANT US TO VACATE RENRIL SO THAT YOU CAN PLACE YOUR ARMY HERE?
OUR NOKKER COUNTER-MEASURES ARE ALREADY PERFECT.
DO YOU SPEAK OF THE MOAT AT THE CASTLE GATES?
YOU WILL NOT DE-FEAT THESE NOKKERS WITH THAT.
...
ILLNESS HAS CONFINED MY FATHER TO BED, AND MY BROTHER HAS NOT RETURNED FROM THE BATTLEFIELD...
YES, I HAVE HEARD.
I KNOW WHAT I AM ABOUT TO SAY IS RUDE...
...BUT IF YOU HAVE COME HERE TO TAKE CONTROL OF RENRIL, YOU WILL KNOW MY WRATH.
T-
TAKE CONTROL?! I WOULD NEVER DREAM OF IT!!

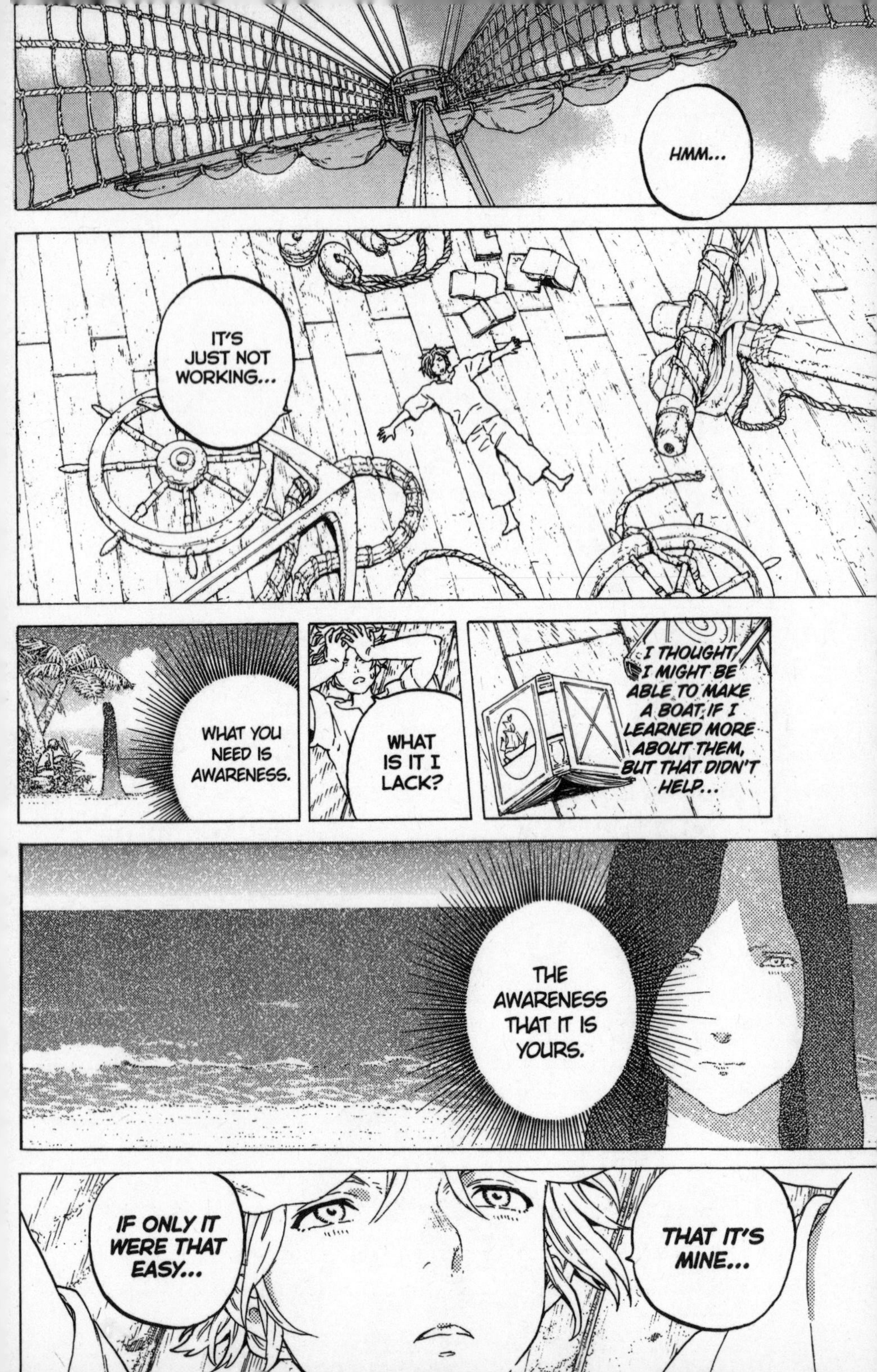
HMM...
IT'S JUST NOT WORKING...
I THOUGHT I MIGHT BE ABLE TO MAKE A BOAT IF I LEARNED MORE ABOUT THEM, BUT THAT DIDN'T HELP...
WHAT IS IT I LACK?
WHAT YOU NEED IS AWARENESS.
THE AWARENESS THAT IT IS YOURS.
THAT IT'S MINE...
IF ONLY IT WERE THAT EASY...

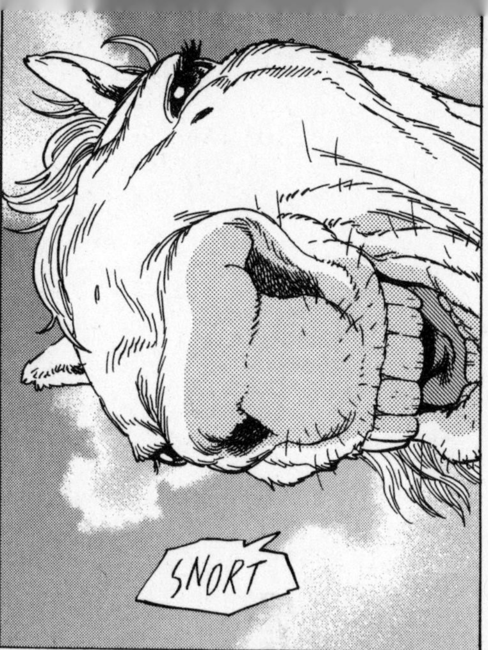
SNORT

WHAT IS IT?
YOU HUNGRY?
HERE.

WHAT'S THE MATTER? EAT IT.
ARE YOU TIRED OF THOSE?
ROLL...

IS THE HAY ON THE SHIP ROTTEN?

...

OH, I KNOW!
WHY DON'T WE GO FOR A WALK IN THE FOREST FOR A LITTLE FUN, HORSE?
WE CAN LOOK FOR FRESH FRUIT OR SOME-THING!

WOOF!
YEAH, THAT FEELS GOOD! THE WEATHER'S NICE, TOO! THIS IS AWESOME!

WOW!
A CITY!
WE'LL FIND HAY AND FRUIT AND EVERY-THING!

SOME-THING SMELLS GOOD!
THIS WAY!

WELCOME! WELCOME!
LOOK! IS THAT FRUIT?
I'VE NEVER SEEN ANY OF THESE!

グリ RUB
グリ RUB

グリ RUB
グリ RUB

COME AGAIN.
RUB RUB

THEY ALL LOOK TASTY.
HEY, PAL, AREN'T YOU GONNA BUY SOMETHIN'?

OH...

OF COURSE I'LL BUY SOME.
A PLEASURE DOING BUSINESS WITH YA!

SIGH... I'VE GOTTA FIX THAT HABIT OF MINE.
THIS IS HOW PEOPLE MAKE THEIR LIVING.

OH!
THAT'S HAY!

CAN YOU SPARE SOME HAY FOR MY HORSE, MISTER?
I CAN PAY YOU.
YEAH, SURE.

ALL RIGHT... I GUESS THAT'S EVERYTHING WE WERE AFTER...
POOR GUY.
IS HE STARVING?
THIS FRUIT I JUST BOUGHT...
EAT THIS... AND FEEL BETTER...
YOU CAN... HAVE THIS...
USE IT TO BUY ANY FOOD YOU WANT.
JINGLE
WHAP
YOU'RE NOT TRICKING ME!!

JINGLE
OH...
I'M NOT GOIN' ALONG WITH SOME RICH BOY'S FUN!

WH-WH-WHAT'S YOUR PROB-LEM?!
I WAS JUST TRYING TO HELP YOU!

YEAH, AND I BET IT FEELS REAL NICE CONTROLLING PEOPLE'S SPIRITS LIKE THAT!

CON-TROLLING...

STMP
TMP
TMP

THAT'S NOT WHY I...
HURRY, HURRY, HURRY! STEP RIGHT UP!

ARE THEY A NEW KIND OF ANIMAL?! OR ARE THEY HUMAN?! DEEP IN AN UNEXPLORED FOREST, I CAPTURED A PAIR OF THE FAMOUS DOKI, THE LEGENDARY EARTHENWARE PEOPLE!!

WHAT THE...?
I FEEL PAIN COMING FROM IN THERE...

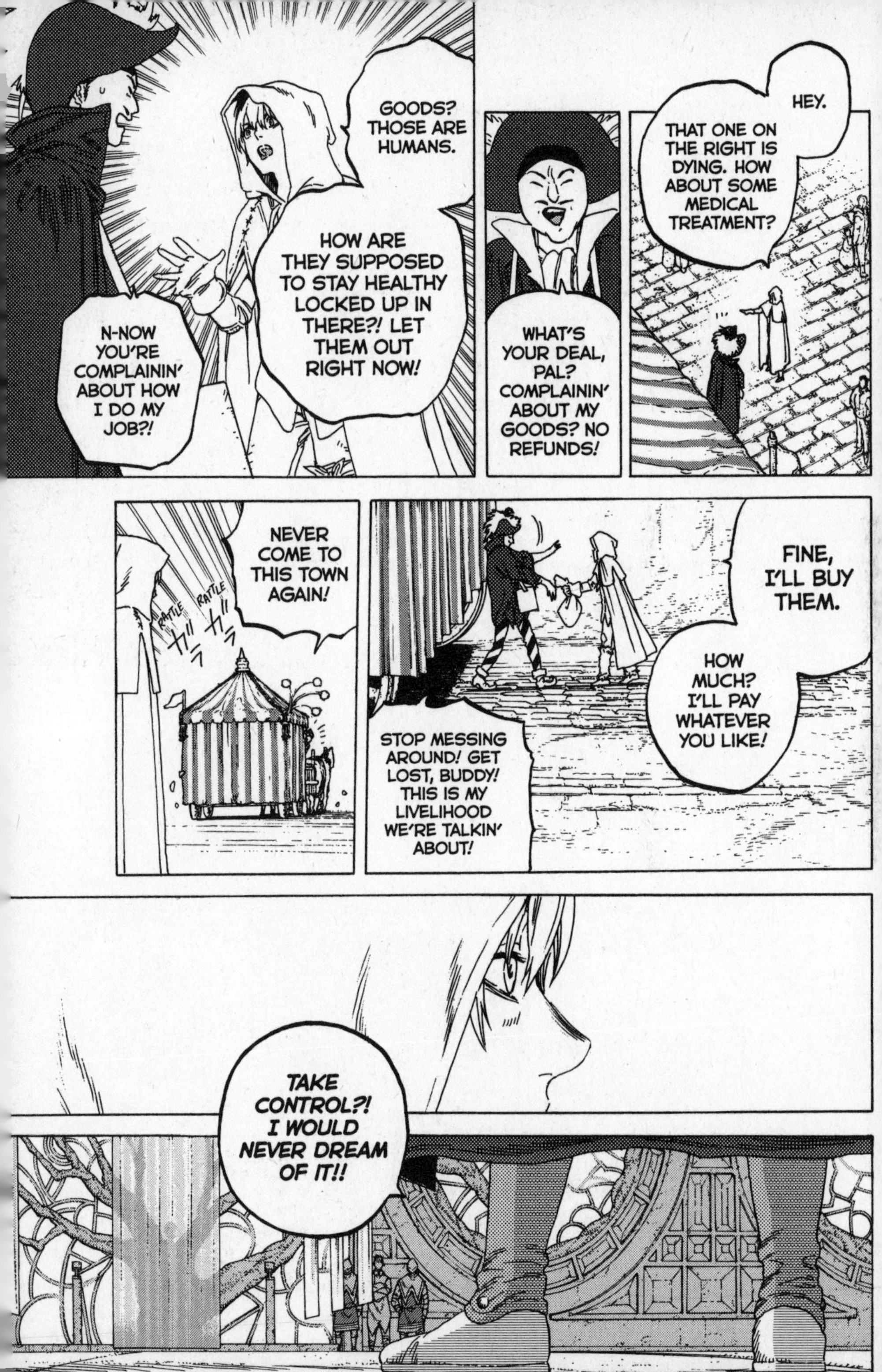
HEY.
THAT ONE ON THE RIGHT IS DYING. HOW ABOUT SOME MEDICAL TREATMENT?
WHAT'S YOUR DEAL, PAL? COMPLAININ' ABOUT MY GOODS? NO REFUNDS!
GOODS? THOSE ARE HUMANS.
HOW ARE THEY SUPPOSED TO STAY HEALTHY LOCKED UP IN THERE?! LET THEM OUT RIGHT NOW!
N-NOW YOU'RE COMPLAININ' ABOUT HOW I DO MY JOB?!
FINE, I'LL BUY THEM.
HOW MUCH? I'LL PAY WHATEVER YOU LIKE!
STOP MESSING AROUND! GET LOST, BUDDY! THIS IS MY LIVELIHOOD WE'RE TALKIN' ABOUT!
NEVER COME TO THIS TOWN AGAIN!
RATTLE RATTLE
TAKE CONTROL?! I WOULD NEVER DREAM OF IT!!

I BELIEVE A FUTURE IN WHICH YOU FIGHT AGAINST THIS THREAT AND SURVIVE IS PREFERABLE TO ONE IN WHICH YOU MAY DIE!

AND I KNOW HOW TO FIGHT IT!

I UNDER-STAND WHAT YOU MEAN.

BUT I WILL NOT GIVE YOU THIS CASTLE...

...OR THE CITY.

YOU WON'T... EVACUATE?

...THAT WE FIGHT THE NOKKERS AND DEFEND THE PEOPLE TOGETHER!
I SHALL HUMBLY WORK...
...TO WIN YOUR TRUST.

CLANK
ガ

COME ON.
I'LL TAKE YOU HOME.

HOLD ON.

CLOP
CLOP

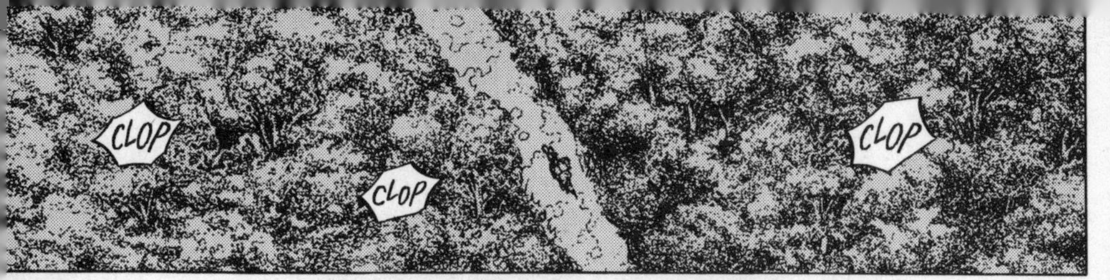
CLOP
CLOP
CLOP

CLOP
CLOP

CLOP
CLOP

CLOP
CLOP

I'M SORRY... I COULDN'T SAVE HIM...

WAS HE YOUR BROTHER?

...

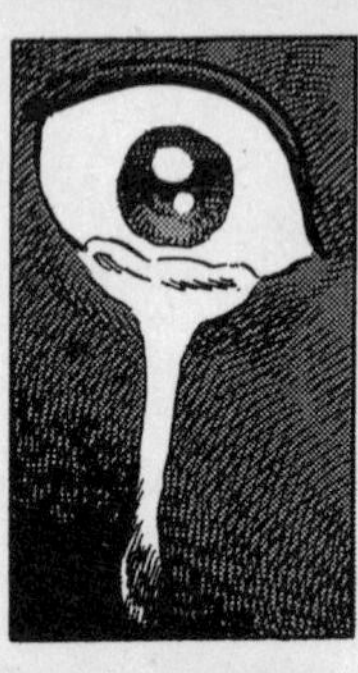

I'LL DO...

...THE BEST I CAN...

GASP!

#84 Resonance

くんくん
SNIFF SNIFF

...

ISN'T THAT GOOD?
THAT'S URALIS COOKING.

...
SO, WHAT'S YOUR NAME?

D-
DO YOU KNOW WHERE YOU CAME FROM?

...

...
YOU DON'T UNDERSTAND WHAT I'M SAYING?

ドス
THUNK

...

Y-
YEAH.

YOUR BROTH-ER? DIED...
OF COURSE YOU'RE NOT DOING ALL RIGHT...

...

I KNOW.
ワ
TUMP
DO YOU LIKE ANIMALS?
ワ
POOF!
HOW DO YOU LIKE THAT?
I CAN TURN INTO ALL KINDS OF THEM!
RUSTLE!
ガサ!
SHWIP!

THIS IS A DONKEY.

OH, LOOK! THERE ARE CHICKENS OVER THERE.
OH! A KITTY!

DO YOU KNOW WHAT KITTIES ARE?

'IDDY!

...OH, SO YOU *CAN* TALK?
NOT "IDDY," "KITTY." *KITTY.*

'IDDY!

...

THEN I'LL CALL YOU "IDDY."

FOR SOMEONE WHO CAN'T EVEN UNDERSTAND THAT GIRL CORRECTLY, AM I REALLY EVEN EQUIPPED TO RE-CREATE THIS BOAT?

WHAT... SHOULD I DO WITH HER?

SNIP SNIP

I'VE GOTTA BORROW THIS, REAN.

I'LL AT LEAST GET HER SOME CLEAN CLOTHES.

FWIP FWIP

BUT I GUESS SHE NEEDS A BATH FIRST...

SCRUBBA
SCRUBBA

FWOOM
CLACK!

COME HERE, IDDY.

キャ
EEK!
キャ
EEK!
キャ
EEK!

SPLOOSH!

NOW YOU'VE DONE IT!

グイ
YANK

ジャキ
SNIP

YEP!
GOOD! VERY GOOD! I THINK THAT'LL WORK.

CONTROLLING PEOPLE!!

STARE...
じ...

は GASP!

Y-YEAH, THAT'S GOOD, HUH?
I'VE GOT SOME STUFF TO TAKE CARE OF.
WHY DON'T YOU PLAY OVER THERE?

SPLOOSH
ザァー

CONTROLLING PEOPLE? THAT'S RIDICULOUS.

DID MARCH SAVE ME IN ORDER TO CONTROL ME?
NO.

TONARI?
SHE WAS DESPERATE TO SAVE HER FRIENDS.

BON WAS THE SAME WAY.
HE SAVED A BUNCH OF PEOPLE AT THE COST OF HIS OWN EXISTENCE.

IDDY?!

WHAT'S WRONG, IDDY?!

THROB

IDDY!

DID YOU FALL? WHAT WERE YOU DOING?

O-OH, THERE'S A HOLE UP THERE?

I DIDN'T NOTICE...

WERE YOU TRYING TO FIX IT?

IT FEELS LIKE
THEY WERE
PART OF ME
THE WHOLE TIME.

IN THAT
CASE...

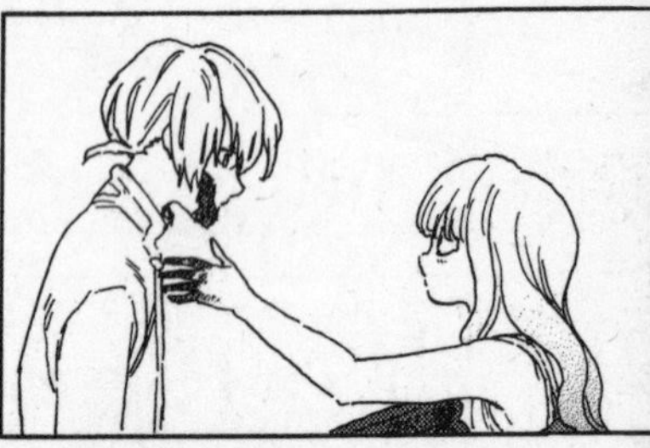

SHWIP

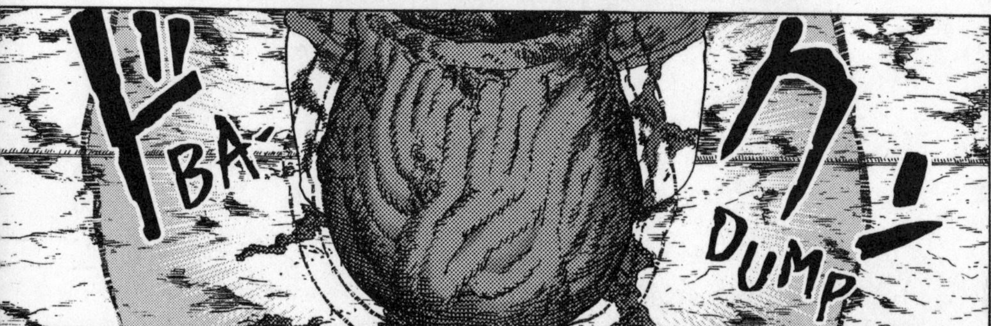
ド
BA
ク
DUMP

WHAT THE?
SOMETHING'S...
...FLOWING INTO ME FROM THE POT?

ARE THESE...

...FEELINGS OF CONCERN FOR ME?

WHILE IT MAY BE HARD TO UNDERSTAND AT FIRST, ONE DAY WE'LL BE ONE.
RIGHT NOW, I HAVE TO APPLY THAT FEELING TO THIS PLACE.
LET'S DO THIS.

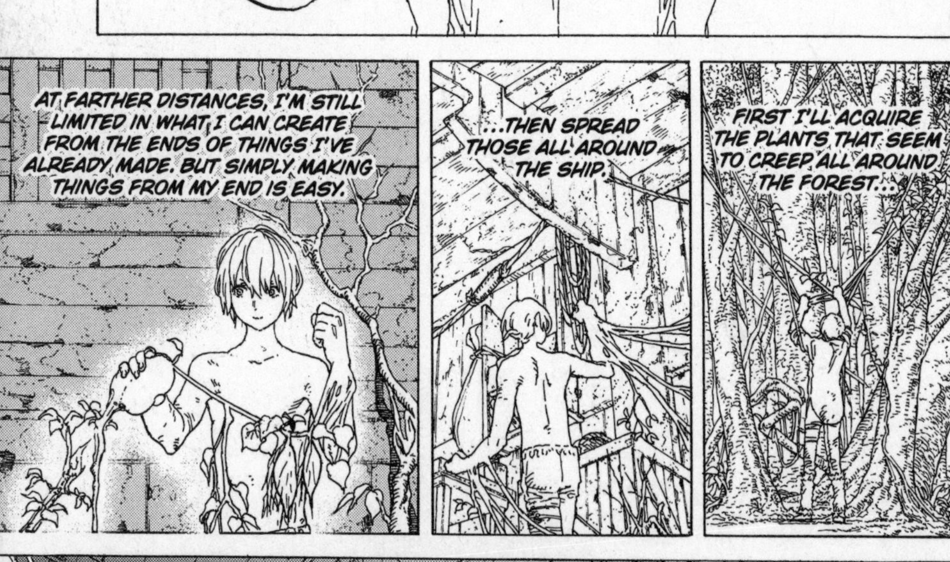
FIRST I'LL ACQUIRE THE PLANTS THAT SEEM TO CREEP ALL AROUND THE FOREST...
...THEN SPREAD THOSE ALL AROUND THE SHIP.
AT FARTHER DISTANCES, I'M STILL LIMITED IN WHAT I CAN CREATE FROM THE ENDS OF THINGS I'VE ALREADY MADE. BUT SIMPLY MAKING THINGS FROM MY END IS EASY.

I HAVEN'T EXACTLY BECOME ONE WITH THE SHIP...
...BUT I THINK IT WILL HELP ME FEEL THE SHIP BETTER.

STOMP
STOMP
IDDY'S RUNNING.

A STORM.

A LEAK?
I DIDN'T NOTICE.

CONCENTRATE.

THE ANIMALS ARE RESTLESS.

RAIN IS POURING IN.

WIND IS BLOWING IN.

THE LEAVES ARE SHAKING.

GWOOP
ギュル

POP
POP
POP
POP

PLOP
PLOP

RUSTLE RUSTLE
バサバサ

SHRP
キッ

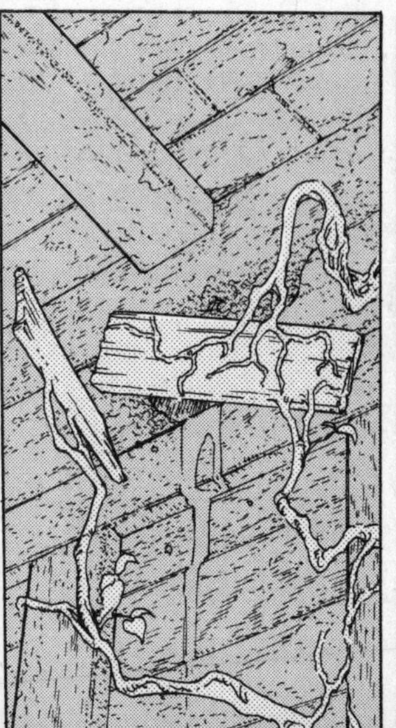

JUST BECAUSE WE HAVEN'T HEARD FROM FUSHI IN TWO WEEKS DOESN'T MEAN WE HAVE TO RUSH BACK TO CHECK ON HIM.
RUSTLE

AREN'T YOU WORRIED, BON?
HE MIGHT HAVE IGNORED YOUR WARNING AND BEEN LOST TO THE NOKKERS ALREADY.

HUFF
STILL...
...THIS FOREST SEEMS ENDLESS.

YES, ACCORDING TO THE MAP, WE SHOULD BE REACHING THE BOAT ANY MOMENT.

A TABLE!
WHAT'S IT DOING HERE?!

WHOA!
HUH?

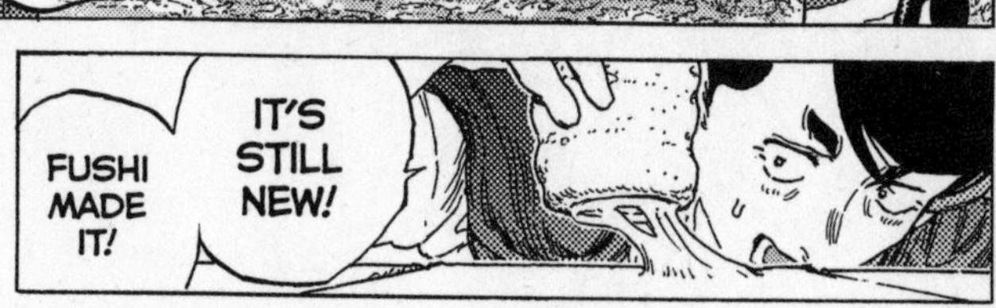
IT'S STILL NEW!
FUSHI MADE IT!

HEY, BON, KAHAKU.

I'M ABOVE YOU.
TAKE THE STAIRS AND JOIN ME.

YOU'VE GOTTA BE KIDDING...
WHAT'S GOING ON HERE?

!!

WOW, THIS IS ALMOST...
...LIKE YOU MADE YOUR OWN LITTLE PLANET, HUH?

To be continued in Volume 10

TO YOUR
ETERNITY

NEXT VOLUME PREVIEW
MORE IMMORTALS LIKE YOU WOULD BE APPROPRIATE.
—"What" Are They?

Those Who Come to Fushi
THE DECISIVE BATTLE WITH
THE NOKKERS APPROACHES —
THE RENRIL ARC BEGINS!

A Kodansha Comics Trade Paperback Original.

Published in the United States by Kodansha Comics,
an imprint of Kodansha USA Publishing, LLC, New York.

Publication rights for this English edition arranged through Kodansha Ltd., Tokyo.

First published in Japan in 2018 by Kodansha Ltd., Tokyo,
as *Fumetsu no Anata e* volume 9.

Cover Design: Tadashi Hisamochi (hive&co., Ltd.)
Title Logo Design: Shinobu Ohashi

ISBN 978-1-63236-734-1

Printed in the United States of America.

www.kodanshacomics.com

9 8 7 6 5 4 3 2 1

Translation: Steven LeCroy
Lettering: Darren Smith
Editing: Haruko Hashimoto, Alexandra Swanson
Editorial Assistance: YKS Services LLC/SKY Japan, INC.
Kodansha Comics Edition Cover Design: Phil Balsman